Bobby Gunn

Autobiography

The Undefeated Bare Knuckle Boxing Champion

TABLE OF CONTENTS

CHAPTER 1
THE CALM BEFORE THE FIGHT

Bobby Gunn is pacing the concrete floor of an auto-body shop amid the industrial wastelands of a huge northern city. "I'm worried," he says, wringing his mallet-like fists. "I've heard this guy today is a head-butter."

More pacing and hand-wringing as Gunn falls deeper into a temporary malaise amidst the garage's taxidermy heads and faded American flags. Today's opponent, a former marine, is known for dropping his head during fights—a common tactic among gloveless fighters who can easily fracture a hand by striking the skull. Gunn has executed the technique several times. He's fractured his right hand just as frequently. Another fracture might mark the end of his career.

"Everybody wants to take me down, brother, and make a name for himself," he adds, smashing through a wall of rubber tires. "I've gotta watch my back."

Whap, whap, whap.

Gunn pounds the tread, keeping his hands slightly open until right before impact, which loosens the knuckles. He has black hair, blue eyes, and 235 pounds of muscle, with a 5-foot-11 frame and a cowboy-like bowlegged walk. Every morning, he gets up at six a.m., shaves with a straight razor and rubbing alcohol, puts on his normal gear (denim jacket, pants, gray Henley, black Pumas, cell phone holster), and does two hundred push-ups. He has no tattoos and doesn't drink. His favorite book is The Bible. "I'm a hugger," he'll say, almost crushing your torso in a complete embrace.

Gunn used to enter matches without cracking a knuckle, but he now requires a warm-up. An extensive one. He is forty-two years old, when most combatants have already retired. He's fractured his right hand six times and dislocated his fingers so frequently that he now resets them with his teeth during matches. He has no cartilage remaining in his nose and can flatten it against his face like a rubber prosthetic. He also shattered two bones in his back, fractured his elbow, and seriously injured his right foot after falling from a two-story roof on a construction job in 2000. After his most recent mishap, which left eighteen screws and bolts in his foot permanently, doctors warned him he would never be able to walk again. Within a year, he was back in the ring, fighting from a different position.

Gunn typically knows what to anticipate from his opponents in the underworld, but soldiers are unpredictable. With professional boxers and MMA fighters, he may expect a serious fight. He can finish it swiftly with neighborhood toughs like bouncers and bodyguards, who are usually washed-up linebackers proficient at kicking frat boys out. But military men are different. They have official training in hand-to-hand combat, but not enough time in the ring to hone their skills. Soldiers are unpredictable, which makes them dangerous. "Anytime you get a marine or army guy, they're usually a stupid ass," Gunn jokes. "They make mistakes. They think with their hearts rather than their heads."

Whap, whap, whap.

Gunn is competing in a lunchtime battle in October 2015, in a run-down area that clings like a lint to the freeway. The auto body shop is a significant distance from Caesar's Palace. It's a massive space with twenty-foot ceilings, oil-stained floors, and tool chests lining the walls. A baby-blue vintage Mustang sits on a hydraulic lift. A wild-eyed bear's head hangs on the wall. In the corner, an industrial fan blows grease-soaked air. The shop's double-bay sliding door is closed, so the only way in is through the cluttered front office, where the owner admits the last few customers, hangs the "Closed" sign, and locks the door.

In the center of the garage, approximately thirty men and one lady form a loose circle. As with most bare-knuckle fights, the crowd is blue-collar: old men with faded tattoos and beer guts, a construction foreman in a polo, and a couple of roofing contractors on lunch break. The lone woman is dressed in a black tank top and cutoff shorts. "This is exciting because it's illegal," one man says.

For this match, the promoter sent a single email to a small group of frequent fight fans. The crowd does not pay a cover charge, but they are gambling. Gunn and his opponent will be paid upwards of $5,000 each. This is less money than Gunn typically earns for a fight, but it is not about the purse. Gunn is the undisputed champion of the underground bare-knuckle circuit, with an unblemished 71-0 record gained in blood from channel docks, freeway overpasses, and mafia McMansion dens. His name is at stake. "I'm going to pick my shots and take him down quickly," he says, breathing steadily. "My record is everything."

Whap, whap, whap.

Gunn growls, accelerating his pace. Punching the tires transports him back to his childhood, to the Shamrock Boxing Club in Niagara Falls, Ontario, where his people, the Irish Travelers, would always return each fall. Back then, Gunn's father would wrap tire tread around a punching bag and make him alternate between hitting the rubber and the leather, working the bag until his knuckles bled and stiffened.

In Niagara Falls, Robert Williamson Gunn, descended from a long series of itinerant brawlers, trained his only son to carry on the family tradition. He told him to rub a leather belt over his brows to toughen them and to apply kerosene to his cuts to speed up the healing process. He taught him how to tolerate pain by covering a baseball bat in foam and duct tape and repeatedly beating his son in the belly to strengthen his abs. Most importantly, Gunn's father taught him to always be prepared for combat. Robert would wake him up in the middle of the night from their hotel rooms and trailer parks, grinning with glassy eyes and a Marlboro Red dangling from his mouth, to fight grown men he had brought home from the bar. He bet up to $1,000 on the kid brawler he had raised since birth. "He would ask, 'Can you beat that boy right there?'" Gunn recalls. "How much would you like to bet?'"

Whap, whap, whap.

Gunn lets out a sharp cry and moves back. He stretches his tree stump neck from side to side. He opens and closes his mouth while moving back and forth on the balls of his feet. "I'm nervous," he admits. "I don't know what he's going to do."

Gunn is accompanied by his trainer, Dominick Scibetta, and his 19-year-old son, Bobby Jr. Bobby Jr. has seen all of his father's fights, from pro boxing matches in 20,000-seat stadiums to gloomy conflicts in abandoned warehouses, and is concerned about how much longer his father can live. "I feel nervous," he adds, his arms crossed, chewing gum, and staring straight ahead. "It hurts my chest."

Dom, an elderly boxer from Boston with tired eyes and a big belly, has other problems. He has been with Gunn through hundreds of underground bouts, witnessed many more over the years, and understands what it takes to win. Most significantly, he understands how little it takes to lose. Dom, a once-promising professional boxer, collapsed when he arrived at Madison Square Garden in 1988, so terrified that he could hardly walk through the crowds after leaving the locker room. His career lasted just a year after that. He understands that Gunn should not be concerned about today's opponent, a relative unknown. But he also understands that in the combat game, anything can happen—especially if you allow for doubt. "Anxiety can break you down," he explains. "But Bobby has coped with it for years and can wash it away. "He is an old-school tough guy."

Dom leans down and places his mouth directly in Gunn's ear. "He's the one who's pacing back and forth," Dom explains, gesturing past the crowd toward the body shop's front office. "He's the one who's worried."

Gunn shook his head. "I don't know."

"Trust me."

Gunn looks towards the door.

He looks back at the tires.

Whap, whap, whap.

Outside the auto-body business, Gunn's opponent, Jim McClendon, sits in his car and meditates. "Before fights, some guys pray, and some guys do breathing exercises, what I call the 'woo-sa.'" He inhales, holds, then exhales.

"You got to get mentally focused," he tells you. "Or you'll get knocked the fuck out."

McClendon, twenty-eight, is the last person you'd expect to see in a bare-knuckle battle. He is an accountant, a marine, and a doting father to his eleven-year-old daughter. His favorite magazine is The CPA Journal. "I help small businesses who can't afford a private accountant," he jokes. "Have you ever tried to hire someone? "Those guys are expensive."

McClendon stands 6'3" and weighs 200 pounds, a ropy, muscled natural athlete with a handsome face and easygoing demeanor. He wears a white T-shirt, acid-wash pants, and black sneakers. He is the only Black man in the fight today. "Not a lot of Black dudes do this," he shrugs.

After graduating from high school in Philadelphia, McClendon spent a year playing semi-professional basketball in Japan. When the NBA failed to call, he joined the Marines, serving as a corporal with the First Light Armored Reconnaissance Battalion in southern Iraq from 2008 to 2009. He gained two talents there: accounting and fighting. "It's not like the army, where you do just one job," he explains. "If you're a marine, then you're an accountant and a killer, too."

After the war, McClendon returned to Philadelphia, found a CPA job, bought a car and a house, and started helping to care for his eight-year-old daughter, whom he had in high school before he was ready to be a parent. Everything appeared to be on track. But McClendon was tortured. "I have pretty bad PTSD," he says. "It was some shit in Iraq."

McClendon had a nervous breakdown when his platoon's best friend died by suicide. He lost his job, home, and car. He went about as far as a guy can go, destitute and living on the streets for years, planning to see his daughter in public parks. "My PTSD went untreated, you know, because, as marines, we're tough, we don't want to go to the hospital, that's being a pussy, blah blah blah," according to him. "But then, when my best friend killed himself, I was like, 'Maybe I should get some help.'" After a two-year wait, McClendon was admitted to a VA hospital, began therapy, and acquired a loan to rent an apartment. He parked cars to pay the bills and finally launched his own business, handling the books for small and medium-sized firms. He recently shared a photo on Instagram of himself and his now-teenage daughter, both of whom are smiling while going over tax documents at his apartment. "I have a ton of deals to complete, and guess who's assisting me?" the caption stated.

So, after going through such suffering and eventually coming out on top, why on earth is McClendon competing in a sleazy underground bare-knuckle match, risking jail and terrible injury? The solution is difficult. Yes, the PTSD he suffers from derives from the devastation he witnessed overseas. But it's also the result of his worry and melancholy over returning to a sterile world of Costcos and swipe-right binge dating, where everyone messages but no one talks. A world in which complete strangers appreciate him for his devotion yet no one understands the distinction between Sunnis and Shiites. McClendon understands that this sounds crazy, yet he misses war. He misses the ties he formed in combat, where decisions were actually important and he and his unit members lived and died for one another. He misses the combination of adrenaline and purpose, the raw joy he can now only obtain with bare knuckles. "It's weird, but I love to fight," he replies. "I'm no longer a Marine, so bare-knuckle boxing makes me want to fuck somebody up. And it is in the name of brotherhood. People think bare-knuckle boxing is cruel, but the fighters shake hands afterwards."

McClendon witnessed his first underground fight as a Marine stationed at Camp Pendleton, California—a roped-off contest in a nightclub basement. He was fascinated. Now he's aiming to establish his own identity in the sport. So when the promoter contacted him about today's bout—a last-minute call-up, as is often in the circuit—he recognized that it was a unique opportunity. If he defeats Gunn, a man thirty-five pounds heavier, fourteen years more experienced, and with sixty-five more underground victories, he will make money and get immediate celebrity. He'll take the title.

McClendon stops meditating, exits the vehicle, and enters the body shop's front office. Standing among the metal file cabinets and out-of-date calendars, he peers through the shop's dirty interior glass, his gaze drawn to a massive figure in the corner. Gunn.

"It was the first time I'd seen him in my life," McClendon recalls. "He is constructed like a wall. He removed his jacket, and I was like,

'Oh, my God.'"

Even at his middle age, Gunn is a spark plug of muscle and pent-up energy, a bullet with a shaved flat top head. Wearing a black tank, jeans, and sneakers, he looks straight ahead as Dom gets close in his face, muttering orders. Dom, a laconic lug, appears to be going to have a seizure. "Hands high, hands high," he repeats. "Chin down."

Gunn nods, twists his feet, and moves his lips. Dom fakes a blow to the gut before spreading his arms like an umpire signaling a runner safe. Gunn nods. That's it; the fatal shot.

Gunn is courageous in the legal boxing ring, having won twenty-two professional fights, including the 2006 International Boxing Association world cruiserweight title, and facing world champions such as Tomasz Adamek. However, his underground notoriety has made him famous. He's fought for money in every underground venue you can think of, from midtown Manhattan pubs to desert outposts to a Boston gangster den with a caged lion in the corner. He's been carjacked by the Latin Kings, had guns aimed at his head by Russian and Albanian mobs, and robbed at gunpoint by Irish gangsters. Even when bouts turn "rough-and-tumble"—that is, all rules are broken and anything goes—he has never backed down. "I've seen it all," he explains. "Scary things. Men are trying to kill me. Unfortunately, this is the reality we inhabit."

Gunn claims not to be troubled by any of this. "It's nothing to me, pal," he'll reply, shrugging his enormous shoulders. But, of course, this is not true. All warriors become afraid. The fundamental difference is that Gunn does not become concerned about combat until just before it begins. And it is in those moments when the world stops and he looks at his opponent, the man threatening to take everything away from him in a fight that can always turn deadly, that Gunn allows himself to embrace the one fear he harbors deep within his battle-scarred body—that he will somehow fail his family. He reflects on the plain horror he feels every morning as he leads his seven-year-old daughter, Charlene, into the private school he pays for with his bare-knuckle earnings. He hopes the other suburban parents don't find out about his side hustle, and that the world never shuns his little girl for his own faults. "The other parents have no idea who I am," he continues, "and I don't want them to." Gunn stops. "The last thing my little girl told me this morning was, 'Please, Daddy, don't come home with a black eye.'"

Gunn shakes his head and walks to the center of the garage. The hubbub quiets down. The crowd's circle tightens. The only sound is the whir of an industrial fan. Danny Provenzano, an ex-con who did five years in a state jail and is also the grand-nephew of Anthony Provenzano, a crucial figure in Jimmy Hoffa's abduction, looks at the aged fighter.

"Are you ready?"

Gunn nods.

The two men formed a circle. McClendon appears uneasy. He feints and jabs while dancing on his toes, exhaling loudly after each punch. A handful make it, but the most miss. Gunn, on the other hand, has gone through a significant shift. He is calm and serene, his feet firmly planted on the pavement, maintaining pace with his opponent while dodging and weaving with his upper body. He throws fewer punches—sharp jabs primarily to the body—but lands them all. "Oof," McClendon exclaims, shaking his head after taking a hit to the chin.

About a minute into the fight, the guys clinch in a sweaty embrace, regaining their breath, regulating their racing hearts, and assessing one other's tiredness. Then Gunn shoves McClendon away.

The end comes suddenly. Gunn delivers a left hook to the stomach, a right hook to the kidney, and a deadly deep left hook directly to the heart. As his opponent doubles over, Gunn throws a final jab to the chin. McClendon falls. "Pick him up! Get him up!" Gunn shouts, jacked up, and marches back and forth.

On the ground, McClendon shakes his head.

Gunn helps his opponent get up. "Good punch, dog," McClendon comments. Gunn grabs him by the shoulders and stares at him as if for the first time. They both smile and embrace. The struggle is over.

The audience cheers. Gunn is $5,000 richer, but he appears to have just missed his train.

"I'm tired of fighting in the shadows like this," he adds, massaging his knuckles as a mechanic opens the garage doors and brings sunlight into the area.

"I want to make this sport legal."

CHAPTER 2
OLD SCHOOL STYLE

*B*are-knuckle boxing thrives throughout the underworld, from New York to Los Angeles, Moscow, London, and even the cartel regions of Mexico. The sport, like a modern-day gladiator arena, is nearly entirely male, however there are stories of women fighting in bare-knuckle bouts sponsored by the Italian mob on Coney Island. Bare-knuckle fights are essentially boxing bouts without gloves or rounds, and they last until one man drops or swears he's had enough. Fighters dress in regular clothing rather than trunks so they can blend in with the crowd if the cops arrive. The sport is deadly, bloody, and illegal almost everywhere, with motorcyclists and gangland bosses staging fights in warehouses, parking lots, and mafia mansions. "The scene is crazy," Pellegrino says. "There are stabbings and gunshots. Gambling and drinking. People bet on everything. I used to take shots of Jack Daniels before going out. Down south, they occasionally refused to pay, so you had to assert yourself. I remember once knocking out a man who was supposed to be the crap from where he came. His teammates were so enraged with him for losing that they mud-stomped him to a bloody pulp and admitted him to the hospital. He suffered injuries that he never recovered from."

The sport does, however, have one redeeming feature: the winner takes everything. Joey Eye, a Philadelphia cutman and former underground promoter, says, "The blood's red and the money's green."

The circuit is not a formal association. There is no webpage. You cannot acquire access by calling a spokesperson. Instead, it is administered by a loose confederation of regional promoters that monitor prospects, organize fights, and bring in talent from all across the country. Gunn spent years working with Johnny Varelli (now deceased), a matchmaker in New York and Chicago. Gunn was given Varelli's phone number by a gym management in Pittsburgh after winning his first significant underground match—a motorcycle bout—at the age of nineteen. He never met Varelli in person. "You'd call Johnny, tell him you want to fight, and he'd call back a week later with all the details," Gunn tells me. "If you're anybody, they'll know your name."

Bare-knuckle matches are occasionally staged by organized crime, similar to the underground gambling circuits for dog- and cockfighting. (In the Southwest, cartel-funded events frequently feature all three forms of contests.) Small-time producers may also stage events that involve gloved boxing. Sometimes these are spur-of-the-moment financial challenges, with the brawlers' reputations broadcast around the country. "It exists everywhere," says Larry Willis, a former bare-knuckle fighter from Houston. "It's more common in some places—Vegas, Florida, Philadelphia, New York—but it also exists in Colorado, Wyoming, and Indian reservations. There used to be a lot of bustle around here, but hey, maybe I'm older."

New York has long been the core of bare-knuckle boxing, thanks to its high volume of matches, deep boxing culture, and concentrated mix of organized crime and hard-luck contestants, and its feeder system is well-established. Like the fights themselves, Ike's and other hard-bitten Northeast boxing meccas—Champs in Philadelphia, Morris Park Boxing, and El Maestro in the Bronx—are nearly impossible to find. They do not advertise. They don't really have any signs. They are often located in the heart of residential districts, in unassuming row houses that also serve as the owners' homes. However, everyone who follows the local fight scene knows where to find them. In 2008, Brandon Jacobs, a star running back for the New York Giants who had just won the Super Bowl, parked his sports car outside Ike's, stationed a bodyguard nearby, and strolled inside the metal door, donning fighting gloves. Jacobs, a former amateur heavyweight from Napoleonville, Louisiana, was eager to put his abilities to the test. But after a couple of workouts with local boxers, the 6'4", 265-pound behemoth was knocked to one knee by Gunn's left jab to the body and hasn't been seen since. Even an NFL star used to bone-crushing tackles from 330-pound lineman couldn't handle Ike's. (Other fighters at Ike's confirmed this tale, but Jacobs declined repeated interview requests.) "Guys don't know Bobby's a pro," trainer Ray Henderson says with a gold-toothed grin. "But he's a force to be reckoned with."

At some underground fights, over a hundred fans will pay up to $100 per person to gamble on numerous battles, with security patting down entrances and beer and liquor distributed at makeshift bars. At others, a tiny group of fans will gather at the last minute. Regardless of the location or the prize money, at least one person will be familiar with Gunn, the first recognized bare-knuckle boxing champion in the United States in more than 120 years—a renowned brawler who has fought his way through the underground for decades. "There's only one champion of bare-knuckle boxing," world heavyweight boxing champion Tyson Fury declared in a 2016 Twitter video. "And that's Bobby Gunn."

At Ike's, Gunn rounds the hundred-pound bag, pushing and teasing it before destroying it with a barrage of blows, shouting out with each one. "Bop-bop-bop-bop-bop!" "Ay, ay, ay, ay!"Max, Gunn's French bulldog, is chewing a sock a few feet away. Bobby Jr. works a speed bag in the corner, keeping time to Kendrick Lamar on Ike's boom box, and the gym is a whirlpool of pulsating bass, swinging sledgehammers, and gloved jabs. "Do you smell that?" asks Ike's manager, Ossie Duran, a dreadlocked Ghanaian immigrant and middleweight fighter. "It smells like sweat." "It smells of war."

Gunn is gigantic, muscular, the biggest he's ever been, and claims to be on top of his game. However, there have been rumors in the underground that he is aging, that he is no longer the top fighter on the circuit, and that his era is coming to an end. "I would never say this to Bobby, but I can tell he's slowing down," says an underground promoter. "He has transformed the way he fights. He can still hit like a horse and pull off unbelievable side shots that no one sees coming, but he isn't the same. "He is slower."

Gunn has responded. "Nobody's beating me, pal," he says, clutching the swinging bag. "I'm doing a young man's game but take care of myself—God is good to me."

Gunn was raised on the freezing shores of Niagara Falls by Irish Travelers—a nomadic tribe of people who avoid the outside world, speak their own language, and devote themselves almost entirely to family, religion, and fighting—and has made his way with his two fists since quitting school in the second grade. When his pro boxing career flopped, he began earning a living by laying asphalt and waging bare-knuckle bouts in the quick-cash underworld, working out every day while raising his family. Now, from his phone at Ike's, he schedules flights from Los Angeles to Texas and Florida, as well as innumerable contests in his own backyard. He once met two Russian mobsters from Brooklyn at a local Starbucks. "They said, 'We pay you very financially,'" Gunn recalled. "Lovely gentlemen."

In the underground, Gunn is a fabled figure, a ghost, a man famed for his undefeated bare-knuckle record and 40,000 Twitter followers but, until recently, rarely seen except on a handful of blurry YouTube videos. "He becomes almost mythical," says Steve Janoski, a newspaper reporter in New Jersey who watched Gunn fight in a warehouse match in 2011—a bout that has since been viewed online over 1.2 million times. "It carries more weight because you don't know exactly what. You only know the bare bones. Even his name suggests he was born to do this—you can't be an accountant with a name like Bobby Gunn."

Gunn knocks opponents out with his precision blows, which are bare-knuckled and penetrate deeper than gloved attacks, directly to the internal organs. Unlike gloved boxers, who wear thick sixteen-ounce gloves and may thus strike as frequently and as hard as they want, Gunn and other bare-knuckle fighters must punch with less force to prevent breaking their hands, focusing solely on specific portions of the body to avoid hitting hard bone. As a result, Gunn's bare-knuckle battles are more like duels, with each man waiting for the right moment to strike. "Bobby Gunn is a very skillful guy in bare-knuckle boxing," says Joe Rogan, a pundit for the Ultimate Fighting Championship. "I enjoy watching him fight." He avoids throwing full-power punches since they would break his hand. So he chips away at men and breaks them down. When you see him battle, you can know he's been at it for a while. What Bobby Gunn is doing is actual boxing."

Gunn, who can pinpoint the exact pressure areas needed to fall an opponent, begins by attacking the eyes, opening cuts to bloody the eyesight, then striking behind the ears to disrupt balance. He then punches his opponents' forearms, causing them to drop their hands. He avoids the hard bone of the forehead and instead shoots for a three-inch gap between the eyes and the upper lip, steering clear of his opponent's teeth, which can cut skin and cause infection. The chin is fair game but still relatively hard, so he focuses on pressure points along its side and up to the ear, frequently throwing a corkscrew punch, twisting his wrist at the last moment to strike his opponent knuckle-first and better tear the skin, resulting in less trauma to his hand while still delivering a knockout blow.

Mostly, however, Gunn just works the body, rotating to strike opponents from both the front and back, punching deep into the kidney, liver, and heart with the precision of a sniper, inflicting excruciating pain. "It's like getting hit with a ball peen hammer," Janoski explains. "A liver shot feels like your ass drops out of your ass." All the while, Gunn must guarantee he never truly kills an opponent—jail time looms over his head, and the thought of his daughter, Charlene, is never far from his thoughts. While sparring, Gunn occasionally wears boxing trunks decorated with the Star of David—an acknowledgement not of the Jewish religion, but of the little future king who defeated the enormous Goliath with a single precise hit to the head. "The idea is to break a man down without breaking yourself down," Gunn reflects. "I'm like a surgeon."

Surprisingly, Gunn credits bare knuckles for keeping him healthy. While skin-on-skin contact may cause more blood and superficial wounds, as well as a more gruesome appearance, using less force overall appears to result in fewer concussions and cases of chronic traumatic encephalopathy (CTE), a neurodegenerative disease common among former boxers and NFL players. A two-year study published in the Physician and Sports Medicine journal in 2021 discovered that bare-knuckle fighters suffered more lacerations and hand fractures but fewer concussions than gloved boxers. "Intuitively, it makes sense that BKF might not necessarily increase concussion risk, as the absence of hand padding may reflexively make fighters more selective about where they land their punches or lead to less force being administered with each strike," stated the study's authors. Bare-knuckle fighters hit each other with less force than contestants do in either of the other two sports. "Out of boxing, MMA, and bare knuckle," says Randy Gordon, a former athletic co. "Believe me, at my age, I'm taking MRIs," he says, breathing hard and assessing the swinging bag. "And don't think I don't care about those head scans. But I haven't had any signs of a concussion. I was taught the long-forgotten art of rolling your head and shoulders with the shot. People believe that using bare knuckles is primitive, however it is actually safer. This is not a barroom brawl. This is a whole other type of art. It's what has kept me in the game so long."

Gunn's fellow fighters at Ike's regard him as something much more scary than a bare-knuckle knockout artist: a good person. He demolishes sparring partners in the ring before sitting them down to ask if they have accepted Christ into their hearts. He is a family man who arrives every morning with Bobby Jr. and Max, a papaya-sized dog who would look right at home in a Rodeo Drive purse, and then teaches opponents how to elbow them when the official isn't watching. He is a middle-aged Scotch-Irishman who goes out of his way to train brutally with fighters half his age in a predominantly Black gym in a Black neighborhood ruled by the Paterson Bloods, and then sits back with them to discuss career options, family advice, and how he has overcome oppression as a Traveler. "Not many white guys here," says Pierson. "And Bobby is white. For example, he wears stonewashed jeans.

Pierson laughs. But he can fucking fight. I mean, he is vicious inside the ring. He was demonstrating moves like how to catch a guy with an overhand right and finish with a small tip of the elbow. I was like, 'This is nasty.' And he responded, 'No, dude, my blood is gypsy. This isn't dirty. This is fighting.' And when he walked out of the ring, he was a kind teddy bear. When I was going through custody issues with my four children, he would give me a pep talk and never judge me. I heard him speak, and it was constantly about peace and God, and I thought, 'There's something wrong with him.'"

Gunn is sweating profusely today at Ike's. He lifts 120-pound barbells and jumps rope, as well as more unusual bare-knuckle workouts like hoisting rope-tethered weights from his clenched teeth to strengthen his neck muscles, massaging Epsom salts and rubbing alcohol onto his brow to tighten the skin against cuts, and soaking his clenched hands in buckets of dry ice, squeezing them in subzero temperatures to harden the muscles and tendons. He sometimes puts on a World War I-style gas mask to imitate altitude training, wearing it until he nearly collapses and gulps air. He exercises in the same way he fights, with a Styrofoam cup of Dunkin' Donuts coffee by his side. There's no stretching. No water. Sometimes he doesn't even bother changing out of his jeans. Today, however, he wears a black tank top, black shorts, and ten-year-old black high-top boxing shoes that stretch halfway up his shins. Today, he is preparing for battle.

Gunn steps back from the bag, puts on his clothes, and scoops up Max, holding the tiny puppy like a football as he walks past the snarling pit bulls. No shower. There is no warm-down. Gunn needs to move quickly if he wants to make it back for his second workout later today.

In recent weeks, Ike's phone finally rang.

Gunn has a new fight.

A tattooed, teenage boxer approaches. "Whoa," he exclaims, appreciating Gunn's sneakers. "Those are old-school."

Gunn smiles, sweat shining on his face, as the pit bulls pull on their chains.

"I'm old-school."

CHAPTER 3
THE FIGHTER'S HUSTLE

*G*unn is up at dawn six days a week, cruising for jobs in his truck, a black extended-cab Z71 with paving equipment in the bed, ladders strapped to the top, a chrome Jesus fish on the tailgate, and the slogan "Power Washing Roofs and Driveways: Protective Coatings for All Surfaces" in big block letters alongside an American flag on the back window. Max sits on his lap. Bobby Jr. sits shotgun. On the doors, golden metal decals shaped like New Jersey proclaim "Serving the Tri-State Area for Over 20 Years." Gunn removes them at night, cleaning away the bug splatter and storing them in a protective sheath.

"I'm a clean freak," he says, leaving Ike's and heading to his morning job. "I wash this truck inside and out twice a week."

This is Gunn's office, where he works for the majority of the day. The truck's inside included a wallet-size photo of his family seated around a shopping center Santa Claus, a wooden baseball bat, a pair of championship boxing belts stashed behind the seat, and a little bottle of Listerine, which he occasionally gargles and swallows. At stoplights, he takes out a straight razor and shaves his face in the rearview mirror without shaving cream, then pats his skin with rubbing alcohol. Aspirin bottles are ubiquitous, and Gunn prefers pain medicines, homemade whiskey and cough syrup (the only time he consumes alcohol), and extracting his own teeth and setting his own bones to modern treatment. "Who's going to hire me for a job if they see a cast on my hand?" he said. The SiriusXM channel is permanently set to the Elvis station, with Gunn occasionally joining in. Return to the sender! "Address unknown!" Coffee cups and Pepsi bottles abound. Gunn never drank water. "I got tired of it," he admits, shrugging.

While driving, Gunn is constantly fielding calls and tweets from boxers, promoters, lawyers, haters, and fans alike. At one time, a man identified as "Tony the Rhino" calls. "You're nothing but a big sausage!" Gunn laughs as he greets. He paused, his expression suddenly serious. "Was he being a cunt?" Whether it's praise, a fight offer, or a death threat, Gunn answers every call with an earbud dangling from the left side of his face. Every day, he checks in with his father, Robert Williamson Gunn. "Are you okay, old boy?" Gunn will ask.

Robert lives alone in a room at the Three Diamond Inn, an ancient one-story motel in Niagara Falls, Ontario. To contact him, Gunn dials his room number, waits three rings, hangs up, and then calls again right away. Only then will Robert pick up, knowing it's his kid and not one of his local adversaries. To put it simply, his connection with Gunn is difficult. For years, Robert withheld affection from his only child, viciously preparing him as a warrior but never offering him praise. They are currently engaged in a different type of warfare. A hardened bare-knuckle brawler, the 72-year-old widower recently punched out a man thirty years his junior in a bar. In addition, after collapsing on a construction job, he has returned to drinking. Gunn is attempting to return him to God. "When my mom died, my dad actually died," Gunn explains. "He has never been the same. So I pay him a visit, give him a haircut, clean the bottles in his room, and tell him, "Come on, old boy; I got big things cooking."

Gunn is scheduled to work an asphalt-sealing job in Bayonne, New Jersey. As an independent contractor, he hustles for any work he can get, and he's currently on the phone with today's client, a man who claimed he wanted his mother's driveway sealed. "Hello, Robert Gunn here," Gunn says before leaving a message. "We can go to your mother's house right now. "Please call."

Gunn has worked six days a week since leaving school in the second grade, doing everything from painting grain silos to banging nails, but his actual skill, like his father and grandpa before him, is sealing asphalt. Gunn's prized possession is a heavy-duty aluminum box the size of a dog's coffin, full with the black tarry liquid he uses to tack-coat and weatherproof roads, driveways, parking lots, roofs, and chimney flashings. It is a humid, scorching, and exhausting job. Gunn applies the hot rubberized coating by hand, spraying, pouring, rolling, and brushing it into asphalt cracks while avoiding low-hanging electrical cables and irate dogs. He rarely uses dust masks or protective gloves. He nearly died after falling off a roof, an incident that permanently affected his fighting style. "I landed on my left heel, bone fragment shooting out my toenail," Gunn tells me. "Blood was everywhere, squishy, so I took a bungee cord off my ladder rack, wrapped my foot, and then waited on the ambulance."

In 2016, after driving halfway across the country to work with Travelers headquartered in Texas, Gunn and another Traveler pulled into a ranch outside Fort Worth to see if they needed any paving, only to be attacked by a posse of gun-toting men. "It was a father and his bunch of young bucks trying to be wiseguys," according to Gunn. "They felt they were going to pull a bluff on me, and I didn't take it well. I told one of them I'd break his jaw, and the Traveler boy beside me got out and said, 'Do it, and we'll have an OK Corral gunfight, because I'll pull my revolver.' Even if he did not have a gun." Gunn laughs. "Anyway, they laid down the guns, and I fled the area. They do not play in Texas, sweetie."

Gunn has fought throughout his subterranean career while working construction, taking up underworld bouts in the mornings, lunch breaks, nights, and even on the way to job sites with other contractors. "One time, we were on our way to paint a house in Union, New Jersey, and Bob said he had to make a pit stop," says Mike Normile, a Traveler who has known Gunn since boyhood. "We pulled into a warehouse, he knocked this guy out with two punches, and then we got back in the van and went and painted the house."

Normile shook his head. "This stuff doesn't bother him—it's just part of what he does."

Today, while waiting for a client call, Gunn stands in front of a run-down shopping complex in Hackensack, New Jersey, and glances at a boarded-up business. "Eight years ago, when this was a cell-phone place, I fought a guy here at eleven thirty in the morning," he recalled. "Beforehand, I sat in the parking lot, drinking coffee and watched my opponent pace back and forth by the shop's back door. Before conflicts, I become focused, and the appearance of a person can set me off. And this guy was a cocky bastard. "A kickboxer."

Gunn drinks his coffee. "It was his problem. When we went to fight, he was too concerned with his legs. So, while he was doing that, I hit him three times in the chin and knocked him out cold. Boom. Stiff. I lifted his head, instructed his handler to give him some water, and collected my five thousand. I went outside, got another coffee, and started to work.

Asphalt work and underground brawling are tough ways to make a living that may either break a man's spirit or harden it into a foundation of strength. Gunn is the latter. The Visa may be maxed out and his bank account is down to $369—the odd jobs and bare-knuckle bouts never quite bringing in enough, especially in the aftermath of the recession—but he still pays a dollar tip when buying his Dunkin' Donuts regular with extra sugar at the drive-through. "It's all I can do to keep up with the cost of living," he tells me. "But I've had doors closed on me so many times in my life, I like giving back—I know people appreciate it."

Gunn's whole income goes toward one goal: providing his family with the childhood he never had. The Gunns travel everywhere together, including paddle-boating with the swans in Central Park, viewing Pixar movies at the mall, and attending Baptist church at 7:00 a.m. on Sunday. Gunn's family now resides in a neat apartment complex wedged between a Home Depot and the New Jersey Turnpike, rather than the caravan parks he used to frequent as a child. Gunn has been married to his wife, Rose, a blond Traveler from Florida, for 22 years. She has never condoned her husband's fights and dislikes seeing him hurt, which Gunn understands.

"It tells me how much she loves me, she doesn't come," he elaborates. "It keeps me grounded." Bobby Jr., a promising middleweight boxer, stays at home, works asphalt, and trains alongside his father. "My dad is involved in every aspect of my career," he said. "He's my manager, trainer, promoter—everything." Finally, there is pigtailed Charlene, the only family member capable of entirely dominating her father. "I always get told, 'Daddy, you do this and that,'" Gunn adds, smiling. "God help the boy that gets her."

Every weekday morning, Gunn drives Charlene to a private Baptist school, where she talks about her classes and friends. He can't afford the school's $800 monthly tuition, but he enjoys seeing her walk in wearing her uniform—just another typical suburban kid. Gunn can only sign his name with an X, and he does not want his two children to do the same. "I've always dropped off my children at school because I never had that growing up," he tells me. "My little girl gives me a hug before going to bed. She has a little room with all the wee things she enjoys." He pauses. "That's exactly what it is about. "That is what I fight for."

On a recent morning, Gunn was taking Charlene to school when a startling topic arose: bullying. Charlene, four feet tall with freckles, auburn hair, and a pink ballerina backpack, is a sweet girl who adores her friends, her guitar and keyboard piano, and her father, whom she clings to wherever they go. But, like the rest of the Gunn family, she can be a tough negotiator, never giving in, whether it's youngsters on the playground or her own gospel-spouting father. This morning, there were several pressing problems to settle during the fifteen-minute drive: the tooth fairy, who had recently visited,

Charlene's new favorite song, "God of Angel Armies," a modern Christian pop tune she could perform on guitar, and the frequently recited Pledge of Allegiance. And then Charlene, feet dangling over the side of Gunn's backseat, a gap in her front teeth, moved on to another matter that had been bothering her: a bully. "John is a bad kid," she added, furrowing her brow. "He never listens to the teacher."

"She wants me to fight him," Gunn replied with a tense smile.

Gunn uses his gains to keep his family in their comfortable apartment, to go on infrequent fishing excursions upstate, and, most importantly, to pay for Charlene's $9,600-per-year schooling. "Am I broke doing it?" he inquired. "Yes. And it's worth it, brother. At the end of the day, what is the point of becoming a champion if you can't do that for your family?"

Being a blue-collar dad with a secret illegal night job is not easy. Sometimes, on the drive to school, the conversation turns to Gunn's battle. Charlene does not like them. "Mommy gets upset, and it makes me upset too," she reports. "Sometimes he gets punched and sometimes he gets cut, but I know he'll be safe."

Gunn, on the other hand, enjoys the sense of strength and routine that combat provides in an otherwise uncertain world. But he doesn't enjoy his fury, preferring to keep that aspect of himself aside from his family. "I don't like the feeling," he adds about releasing the "monster" in the ring—which is only partially accurate. "My granddad always said leave the bums at the gym. If you fight the monster long enough, you become the monster, therefore I separate my life—I want to immediately return to my family and pretend nothing happened." More importantly, he is concerned that his actions may affect his daughter, upsetting the fairy-tale childhood he has worked so hard to build for her. "It's hard when I walk into the school and see the other parents," adds the man. "If they knew who I was, they wouldn't treat me like a normal person—'Oh, my God, this guy is ferocious.'" But that is not the case.

Gunn promised his wife, Rose, that this would be his final year in the ring. He has consistently breached his pledge. However, at forty-three, he acknowledges it's getting more difficult. "My body doesn't heal the same way anymore," he admits. "My hands are breaking. My joints are wearing out. Every night, when I wake up, my shoulders feel out of place. I have to spin them thirty times in the shower every morning just to get started—I can't lift my hands above my head."

Despite his injuries, Gunn knows he needs one last fight, a match that would help set his family up for a better future, a win that will allow him to expand his construction business and ultimately escape the underground for forever. He hopes that it has finally arrived. "For years, I beat everybody they put in front of me," he jokes. "Now I don't care any more—I've got one more fight and then I'm out."

CHAPTER 4
NO RULES, NO LIMITS

*M*y introduction to the subterranean was a text. For a year, I had been interviewing Gunn, seeing him in gyms and at job sites in New Jersey, until one Thursday in June 2012, he unexpectedly issued an invitation to an upcoming tournament. I was told the battle would take place over the weekend, somewhere in the "NY/NJ area," but heard nothing until the following Tuesday. That morning, around 8:00 a.m., I received another SMS informing that it would take place in Delaware that afternoon. After leaving my job in Manhattan and arriving in the chosen city via Amtrak, I was informed that the flight had been shifted to another state due to them "being on the run" from authorities. I was given a cross street and told it will start in an hour. Good luck.

Driving a rented car in a dreary rain, I arrived at the location, a dilapidated boxing facility in an inner-city district of a big coastal city. Across the street, there was a taxi dispatcher. Around the corner, an undercover cop was making an arrest. In the parking lot, Gunn arrived with a wooden baseball bat draped over his shoulder. "I bring this to all the fights," he remarked, leaning into my car window, rain dripping from his skintight black T-shirt. "Insurance policy."

That afternoon, I witnessed a Hell's Angel knock a marine to the ground in thirty seconds with a shot to the chin and learned my first underground lesson: fights are often the tamest moments of the night, with disgruntled crowd members and entourages occasionally breaking into brawls among themselves. I also learnt the sport's most crucial rule, which explains why this criminal world can thrive in complete secrecy throughout the United States: no one discusses the underground. "This is like betting on a dice game in an alleyway," says Guy Pagan, a boxing promoter and former army ranger who goes to underground fights in Miami. "Bare knuckle is similar to the high I experienced in war. This is our sport; it's real life."

The bare-knuckle circuit has been there for generations, in almost every major city, yet you'll never hear a word about it. In comparison to most sports, it is modest yet deep, as are organized crime and travelers. These are cultures with strong familial bonds that do not welcome outsiders, as evidenced by one of their favorite sports, bare-knuckle boxing. "I'm taking a risk just by talking to you," says Ed Simpson, a Traveler who has accompanied Gunn to fights for decades. "This circuit is unlawful. You're in a warehouse in a bare-knuckle fight organized by the mafia—it's called the underground for a reason."

The oldest bare-knuckle tradition, which still accompanies every match, is a side bet between the two fighting camps. Gunn, like other knucklers, cannot afford to bet $10,000, let alone $100,000, on a fight, so he obtains funds from local gangs or friends and family, always returning twice their investment. "I ain't a rich person, but I know he's going to win, so I'll take a few grand and bet it on him," says Mike Normile, a Traveler calling from a fracking field in North Dakota. "And I've never lost." In the weeks leading up to a bare-knuckle fight, Gunn and his opponent will pay "kick-in money," maybe 20% of the total purse, to a trusted third party to retain as a deposit to demonstrate commitment. On the day of the battle, he and his opponent will hand over the remainder of their stake money, usually a large sum in loose notes, to the house for safekeeping. To guarantee that no one gets any ideas, one promoter claims to carry a "cage," which is a portable metal safe with holes drilled into its lining. When he arrives at the location, he opens the safe, screws it through the back into joists in a wall or bolts it into a concrete floor, and then sets the prize money inside. "We need to provide a certain amount of security," adds the man. "But robbing these places isn't as easy as you may imagine. What are you going to do, stick up 100 guys?"

After a match, the winner gets everything, while the loser must scrape together enough money to reimburse his backers. "He's going to be paying them back with interest," Gunn says of one fighter who loses a fight. "That's how this game goes."

There are fragments of stories concerning the underworld everywhere. Lamon Brewster, a former world heavyweight boxing champion, tells me that his former trainer in Indianapolis, Bill "Honey Boy" Brown, used to "hobo" around the south, fighting bare-knuckle for money in the 1920s. John "Pops" Arthur, a sixty-eight-year-old boxing trainer from Los Angeles, began fighting in underground "death matches" throughout Asia and Africa in the 1960s, brawling with only his bare hands or a thin pair of kangaroo-skin driving gloves. Today, many fighters, including Gunn, Ritch, and Danny Batchelder, a pro heavyweight boxer who used to train with Mike Tyson, participate in the underground for extra money. "It's a different beast from boxing," Batchelder says. "It is more pure. There's no politics, no dishonest promoters or managers, and no corruption. It simply comes down to who is the stronger fighter on that particular day."

Bare-knuckle fight circuits, no matter where they exist, are often linked to organized crime. "I've been to some in Japan," adds Billy Blanks, a former world kickboxing champion. "I was shocked. They were run by yakuza, who had tattoos all over their bodies. They'd open the door to a warehouse and show you Bentleys, Ferraris, females, and rings. I've seen people's legs twisted off—it's horrible stuff.

Although bare-knuckle boxing is now prohibited, it was not always so subterranean. It is possibly the oldest organized sport in existence, dating back to the ancient Greeks, who performed it in their olympiads, believing that fighting represented discipline, bravery, and grace. It appears in the Mahabharata, an epic Sanskrit poem from ancient India, where combatants fought with clenched fists, kicks, and headbutts to honor the gods and kings. During the Roman Empire, the sport was elevated to a national pastime, becoming bloodier, stranger, and more specialized as slaves, soldiers, and even wild animals fought to the death in the gladiators' sand pits. "Next is a boxing bout," Virgil writes in the Aeneid. "From somewhere he produced the gloves of Eryx and tossed them into the ring all stiff and heavy, seven layers of hide, and I sewed lead and iron … You can still see the blood and a splash of brains that stained them long ago." 2

By AD 500, Rome had prohibited all combat sports in the name of Christianity. Bare-knuckle boxing fell into remission for centuries until resurfacing in England in the 1600s and migrating to America two centuries later, producing the first US champion, Tom Molineaux, a 5'8" 200-pound slave from Virginia. There is no hard evidence of Molineaux's early years, and legend has most likely seeped into the historical record, but he is said to have come from a family of fighting slaves, including his father, a noted prizefighter, and that he competed in bouts on plantations for gambling masters from a young age. After winning $100,0003 for his wealthy owner in a high-stakes match around 1804—a sum now valued at $1.6 million after adjusting for inflation—he was given $500 and set free. He promptly moved to New York, where he worked on the docks of the East River—likely competing in illegal fights at Catherine Market—before moving to England at age twenty-five and squaring off against UK champion Tom Cribb, for 200 guineas, near London in 1810. The English champ, a 5'10", 180-po Molineaux, on the other hand, stunned the crowd by knocking Cribb unconscious with a shot to the throat in the ninth round before losing the fight due to foul tactics—at one point, spectators even invaded the ring, possibly severing one of the American's fingers. While Cribb remained a national hero,

Molineaux sank into alcoholism and dissolution, dying of liver failure at the age of 34 in a barracks in Galway. His era of the sport was immortalized by a nineteenth-century journalist as "the sweet science of bruising."

By the 1840s, bare-knuckle fighting had eclipsed horse racing as one of the most popular hobbies in the United States. From 1840 to 1870, the New York press covered boxing and bare-knuckle fighting more than any other sport except baseball. Despite the fact that the fights were illegal, the country's burgeoning newspapers covered them obsessively, and the combatants' techniques were the same as Gunn's today. "Pugilists harden their hands in different ways," says boxing writer Robert K. Turnbull in 1889. "Good firm rubbing is one of the most effective ways to harden the flesh and bones of the hand. The washes used include alcohol, lemon juice, rock salt, gunpowder, diluted saltpeter, tannin, and alum. Jem Carney, the English light-weight champion, used to whet his hands over a smooth plank for hours a day while training, slapping the backs of his hands back and forth over the wood as a man belts a razor." The boxers were careful, usually aiming for the body. "In fighting or boxing, the hands should be held loosely, half open, all the muscles and those of the forearms relaxed, till the moment of delivery, when the fist should be most tightly closed," according to Turnbull. "The pit of the stomach, known as the mark,' was one [among the most vulnerable points for hits], and a hard blow to this area was very telling. Other areas of attack included the buttocks of the ear or the jugular vein, the temples, the eyes, the throat, right above the heart, and the short ribs."

New York was the genuine capital of bare knuckle boxing during its peak, and it still is today. In the mid-nineteenth century, the city was flooded by hundreds of thousands of Irish immigrants fleeing the potato famine—first-generation Americans who quickly became the country's first true sports heroes. By day, these top-hatted toughs worked as tradespeople. By night, they engaged in illegal matches, spilling blood with firearms, knives, and fists in pursuit of their American dreams. These were the real-life incarnations of the characters in Martin Scorsese's 2002 film Gangs of New York. James "Yankee" Sullivan was an Irish convict exiled in Australia who escaped and reinvented himself in Manhattan as a champion prizefighter and saloon owner. John C. Heenan, the 6'2" 200-pound son of Irish immigrants, worked as a porter for the Pacific Mail Steamship Company in San Francisco before becoming a renowned bare-knuckler. John Morrissey, a brutal prizefighter known as "Old Smoke" for once scorching his flesh on a coal fire during a bar brawl, rose above the ring to become a US senator and the founder of the Saratoga Race Course in Saratoga, New York, the country's oldest racecourse. However, no Irish immigrant would achieve more as a bare-knuckle boxer than John L. Sullivan—a plumber, an alcoholic, a womanizer, and a full-fledged billionaire sports celebrity by the end of the nineteenth century.

The son of Irish immigrants, Sullivan was born in Boston in 1858. As a youth, he brawled in Roxbury's streets, frequented saloons, and froze and scalded his hands on rusty pipes. One night, he passed a vaudeville house where a famous boxer was challenging everyone. On a whim, he removed his coat, put on thin gloves, and knocked the man out, sending him crashing backward over a piano. Sullivan, emboldened by his triumph and eager to follow in his father's ditch-digging footsteps, resolved to become a professional fighter. "At the age of nineteen," he wrote in his 1892 autobiography, Reminiscences of a 19th Century Gladiator. "I drifted into the occupation of a boxer."

From the start, the "Boston Strong Boy" was a celebrity. Standing 5'10" and weighing 200 pounds, with cast-iron biceps, dark eyes, and a meticulously curled mustache, Sullivan began his career in 1880, winning match after match on the strength of what newspapers described as his "bull-like rushes" and "sledgehammer right hand." This was a transitional time for prizefighting in America, with gloved boxing beginning to take hold, and "scientific exhibitions of skill" were legal if combatants refrained from heavy hitting—a ridiculous A natural showman, Sullivan would put on skin tight gloves and offer $50 to any man who could enter the ring and go four rounds with him. He defeated a slew of opponents, dropping money on their prone bodies as if leaving a gratuity, while battling in the backs of beer halls, on moonlit barges, and on short tours of towns such as Buffalo, Pittsburgh, Louisville, and Chicago. He gathered larger crowds and joined them in saloons after his victories, buying rounds, fighting, and chasing women (despite his marriage to Annie Bates Bailey, a former prostitute) before returning to his hotel for his traditional breakfast of six dozen clams and a whiskey. In 1882, at the age of twenty-three, he upset reigning bare-knuckle champ Paddy Ryan for $5,000 in a makeshift ring in Mississippi City, a resort town on the Gulf Coast, becoming the most renowned man in America. "My name's John L. Sullivan," he would say, "and I can lick any son-of-a-bitch alive."

Following his bare-knuckle triumph over Ryan, the Boston Strong Boy went on an interminable "knocking-out tour," earning up to $500 each night, sometimes fighting gloved, sometimes bare-knuckle, across America, Australia, Ireland, and even on Baron de Rothschild's chateau in France. He fought in circuses, among clowns, jugglers, and elephants. He fought in Buffalo Bill's Wild West show, alongside cowboys, Native Americans, and mustangs. He flexed his muscles for wax museums, acted in stage plays, promoted beef broth, and was measured and photographed naked by a Harvard doctor obsessed with his "anthropometric" profile. The song "Let Me Shake the Hand that Shook the Hand of Sullivan" was played on piano rolls across the country.

After five years of hard life, Sullivan had become the unthinkable—

soft. He had inflated his frame via excessive drinking, broken his left arm in a gloved contest, and, most damningly, fought to a draw in a bare-knuckle bout in England, calling his championship title into question. On the eve of his 30th birthday, bedridden with drunkenness and his career on the line, Sullivan decided to put it all on the line in one final bare-knuckle combat. After betting $20,000 on a superfight against Jake Kilrain, a Boston mill worker turned champion boxer, Sullivan retired from the spotlight to recover and train in an isolated barn in rural New York. When he emerged two months later, he appeared stronger than he had in years, with only "a small protuberance in the lower belly" remaining from his prior beer gut.

The Sullivan-Kilrain fight, the most famous bare-knuckle fight in American history, was also one of the wildest, most talked-about sporting events of the nineteenth century, with the press continuously hyping it as a tabloid grudge war.

Years earlier, Sullivan had insulted Richard K. Fox, the editor of the National Police Gazette, a popular national newspaper that was one of the first in the United States to have a sports section. Fox spotted the Boston Strong Boy at a restaurant in New York and asked him to his table. Sullivan, on the other hand, suggested that the publisher approach him directly, sparking a years-long public battle. Obsessed with embarrassing Sullivan, Fox began criticizing him in the Gazette, producing defamatory cartoons and editorials about him while also supporting boxers to defeat him. Over the years, Fox scoured the world for heavyweights to face his adversary, including Ryan, Tug Wilson of England, and Herbert Slade of New Zealand. However, Sullivan triumphed over everyone. Finally, in Kilrain, Fox thought he'd found his man, a clean-living slugger who could dethrone the fading legend. For months, Fox carried tales and graphics about the approaching clash, hyping up the public with images of the heroic Kilrain practicing and cuddling kids, while the wicked Sullivan tortured dogs and drank in bars. "Good and evil as typified and contrasted in the lives and habits of two famous American pugilists," declared the National Police Gazette on March 30, 1889. "The Boston Strong Boy and our hero Jake." By the day of the battle, the entire country was waiting for the outcomes, with readers taking sides and betting on their favorite brawlers. "The city is fighting mad," the New Orleans Picayune reported as Crescent City, the chosen staging ground, prepared to host the event. "Everyone has the fever and is discussing Sullivan and Kilrain. Ladies discussed it in street vehicles, men spoke and debated about it in locations where they had never heard the term pugilism before."

The penultimate bare-knuckle title battle of the sport's American heyday was also one of the longest, lasting two hours and seventy-six rounds. Kilrain quickly took the lead, toppling Sullivan with a wrestling maneuver and drawing first blood. In the sixth round, the Boston Strong Boy answered with the bout's first knockdown, a thundering right, bellowing at his ducking-and-weaving opponent, "Why don't you stand and fight like a man, you sonofabitch!" As the audience cheered, the two brawlers settled in. They pummeled each other savagely, stomping feet with spiky cleats, smashing necks and ribs, and slicing faces, their secondary sucking blood from their eyeballs and spitting it out between rounds. Kilrain sipped whiskey. Sullivan, who was meant to be on the wagon, drank whiskey-laced tea before vomiting in the ring. At one point, a part of the newly erected grandstand collapsed, resulting in a tremendous pileup of bodies. Throughout it all, the two men fought until the final round, when, with their skin roasted and burned by the sun, the combat was clearly over. At the start of the seventy-sixth round, a ringside doctor announced that Kilrain was near death. Mike Donovan, one of his cornerbacks, witnessed two guys die in bare-knuckle fights. Kilrain, almost able to keep his head upright, limped toward the scratch as Donovan tossed a damp sponge into the ring. Sullivan had won.

The Boston Strong Boy was now the world's most renowned person, and his win was celebrated from New York to London to far-flung Tahiti. "Sullivan's colors were everywhere about [New York City]," stated a special telegraph from Manhattan to the Omaha Daily Bee on July 10. "At almost all the picture stores, the windows were filled with his portraits." "The bigger brute won," sniffed the New York Times. The celebration, however, was brief. Robert Lowry, the Mississippi governor who had been humiliated for failing to stop the match, offered a $1,000 reward for Sullivan, prompting his arrest in Nashville on his way back to New York. After a lengthy trial, the Boston Strong Boy was found guilty of illegal fighting and sentenced to one year in jail. Eventually, the verdict was reversed, and he paid a $500 fine. Kilrain was arrested and sentenced to two months in prison. Disgusted by the ordeal, Sullivan vowed never to fight bare-knuckle again, instead popularizing gloved fighting under the Marquess of Queensberry Rules, which eventually led to the sport's legalization in 1892 and the birth of modern boxing as we know it.

But bare knuckles never went away. Following Sullivan's death, the sport went completely underground, flourishing in the shadows of America, in illicit gambling dens, far from the headlines it had dominated. Along the way, one group would perfect it as a cultural institution, eventually giving rise to a hero who would one day win Sullivan's belt: Bobby Gunn, a warrior from one of America's most secret groups.

CHAPTER 5
FORGED BY FIRE

*O*n Christmas Day 1973, Jackie and Robert Williamson Gunn were driving south from Niagara Falls, Ontario, to Tampa, Florida, to work for the winter in their red one-ton dual-rear-wheel pickup truck, all their belongings in a sixteen-foot metal caravan behind them, when Jackie's water broke somewhere in rural Appalachian Virginia. The young couple had been trying to establish a family for years, and at one time had to deal with a stillborn daughter. So, when Jackie finally went into labor at a roadside hospital on the day of Jesus' birth, it must have felt like a miracle, a divine sign that their fortunes were changing. Like their messiah, Robert Williamson Gunn III was born in transit. Robert immediately recognized that his son was blessed. "He was a funny-built boy with long arms," says his dad. "I knew he'd be a good banger."

The Gunns were destitute, continually moving from motel rooms to trailer parks and campsites in search of jobs. Beginning in the fall, they lived with his father's kin in Niagara Falls, lodging in wayside hooker haunts with names like the Tropicana, the Blue Moon, and the Three Diamond Inn while enduring Ontario's harsh winters. "I remember sitting in motel rooms and it's thirty below outside, the wind blowing," Gunn tells me. "We'd put a towel under the door to keep the heat in, and I'm sleeping on an old mattress on the floor." In December, they traveled south for a few weeks to visit his mother's family in Tampa, living in a swampy trailer park on the southern edge of town before returning to the frozen motor courts of Niagara Falls. Finally, every spring, they drove their dilapidated caravan from campsite to campsite across Canada and the American midwest, with the young Traveler boy obliged to defend himself from competing tribes and rednecks. It was amid these nameless RV encampments that Gunn learnt to fight. "We had a pretty rough lifestyle," Robert explains. "That's why most of these gypsy kids are a little tougher than the average person—you had to be to survive."

Gunn's parents were Travelers, a migratory tribe located primarily in Ireland and the United Kingdom but also in clandestine, isolated groups throughout the United States. They are deeply devout, segregating themselves based on their Irish (Catholic) or Scottish (Protestant) heritage, and they use Can't or Shelta, a language that is a blend of Irish Gaelic, English, and local slang. In Traveler culture, women are housewives, while men work as laborers—paving, roofing, painting—traveling with the seasons in pursuit of employment. When they have downtime, they fight. "If you have Traveler blood in you, you start going to the boxing gym at five years old," Mike Normile tells me. "This is a tough life, so you need to get used to dealing with hard stuff."

According to Gunn family legend, the clan's first fight in the New World pitted Bobby's paternal great-grandfather, Robert "Black Bob" Williamson, against "Kicking Joe" Watson, a Traveler who earned his nickname for once kicking a lock off a stall to free a trapped stallion, as well as booting a man so hard he died of internal bleeding. Black Bob, named after his raven-black hair, was the first member of his clan to cross the Atlantic, departing from the Scottish Highlands for Montreal in 1915. (Gunn is a mix of Scottish Traveler on his father's side and Irish Traveler on his mother's side.) At the age of nineteen, Black Bob landed in Toronto, working as a horse and mule merchant while also carrying on another family tradition: fighting. "Black Bob was a sparring partner for the sparring partner of world heavyweight champion Jack Johnson," Gunn tells me. "Never beat anybody on the street, either. "Quite a man.""

According to generations of Gunns, Black Bob and Kicking Joe battled on a Sunday afternoon at a Traveler picnic in Toronto in 1917, while the clans were gathering on a meadow after church on their one day off. Watson, a notorious bully, got into a fight with one of Black Bob's brothers, a newly arrived pastor, and poured lemonade on him. Infuriated, Black Bob took off his shirt to defend the family name, facing off against the towering Traveler as a crowd surrounded them. Watson made first contact, kicking Black Bob "near the stones" before the tables flipped and Bob connected with a left hook, pushing Watson into a brick wall and repeatedly laying into him, knocking him unconscious. "My grandfather told me teeth came out of his mouth from the impact," Gunn tells me. "You're not going to beat the Williamson boys."

Robert Williamson, Gunn's grandfather, was born in Toronto in 1919 as one of Black Bob and his wife's eight children. Growing up in poverty during the Great Depression, Robert Senior learned to fend for himself by brawling for money in alleys. "My dad was a street kid," says his son, Robert Jr. "He grew up the hard way, having to fight for everything—best left hook I've seen in my life." After changing his surname to Gunn to avoid confusion with another family of Williamsons who were infamous scammers, Robert senior married and began roaming a thousand-mile circuit in Ontario with his wife and two sons, working asphalt jobs while competing as an amateur boxer and bare-knuckle fighter. He was a pious man of God who donned a button-down shirt and tie even when building roads. "My grandfather never cursed," Gunn explains. "But he also never lost a fight."

Robert senior, a strict disciplinarian and brawler, governed his household like an army barracks. On a frigid February day in the 1960s, a young Traveler arrived at Robert senior's caravan door with two other guys, demanding to fight over a grudge. When Robert senior's wife requested the guys to leave, they insulted her—a serious mistake. "They gave her some cheek," Gunn remembers. "So my grandfather just laughed." Robert senior removed his tie and went into the snow to fight all three men. "The old man is punching, pulling, and swinging when one of them cuts his head with a big saddle ring," Gunn tells me. "So Grandpa struck him with three left hooks, splitting his face like a fish from snout to forehead. "I knocked him unconscious."

Robert senior and the rest of his family excelled at fighting, with one of his nephews becoming a Canadian middleweight champion and knocking out Sugar Ray Leonard in a training camp. But no Gunn would brawl to the extent of his son, Robert Williamson Gunn Jr., a hard-drinking bare-knuckle boxer who broke all Scottish Protestant Traveler law by marrying Jacqueline Marie Lindsay, a lovely dark-haired Irish Catholic Traveler from Tampa. "My grandfather was better with his hands," Gunn said. "But nobody messed with my dad—he was a bad motherfucker."

Robert, born in Toronto in 1943, grew up as a conventional Traveler, leaving school after fourth grade to travel across Canada and the United States with his parents and younger brother in a caravan. "I never really went to school," he admits. "The old lady would put me in class, I'd get shit as the gypsy kid, and then the old man would move us." Robert's brief stint in a classroom was agonizing. "One time, a teacher stood me up in front of everybody and gave me the strap for three days, whacking the fuck out of me," according to him. "Everybody thinks we're the worst." At home, Robert did not do much better. When he was twelve years old, he was badly assaulted by a more experienced bully and returned home with a fractured nose. "I was all cut up, and the old man said, 'You didn't do too well. I cannot have that. "You should go back tomorrow and see the guy again," Robert says, chuckling. "I wasn't getting any pity there."

After leaving home, Robert quickly began wandering on his own, encountering problems along the road. "I loved rock 'n' roll, hot-rod cars, and fighting," he jokes. "I battled in bars and got a lot of glass out of my skull. What can you do, then? It was enjoyable. I enjoyed it." Robert, 5'11" and 235 pounds, with wide-set eyes, thick black hair, and a sly grin, would go on drinking binges for weeks at a time, working tirelessly on jobs and then thinking nothing of blowing everything in a single night, tipping a favorite musician $500 or buying rounds for the house while holding them rapt with stories. Unsurprisingly, money was always tight. "Bobby's father was a free spirit," says Jimmy Ruml, a family friend and traveler from Niagara Falls. "He lived for today." He enjoyed drinking and traveling, and he was popular with everyone. However, he was not accountable for looking ahead to the future. Some folks simply cannot make much money. It might be the alcohol, the lifestyle, or whatever, but no matter what they try, they can't make it."

Robert developed a devastating fighting style. As a young guy in the 1960s, he appeared in over a hundred shows on America's fledgling pro wrestling circuit, which was an early no-holds barred version of the present WWE. Robert toured as "Black Bart," a heel, performing high-flying feats and body-slamming theatrics alongside fellow Ontario wrestlers such as Tony "Cannonball" Parisi. The men traveled in vans, staying in motels and dining at drive-ins while doing violent, bloody concerts in municipal gyms and arenas across North America. "Get the images of Hulk Hogan and spray tans out of your head," Gunn tells you. "My father and these men weren't like the WWE today. These guys were hard old bastards with cauliflower ears and broken necks flying thirty feet in the air, landing on the cement, and then going to the bars." On the wrestling circuit, Robert faced legends like Bruno Sammartino, a head-pounding muscleman, and Fritz Von Erich, a merciless former college quarterback who once broke his ankle after being flung sixteen feet from the ring. "Yes, my dad and those guys were actors who knew who was going to win and who was going to lose," Gunn replies. "But many a night, they would get a few drinks in them, decide not to cooperate, and begin wrestling for real, blood pouring out of them, breaking bones." Robert, who was already seasoned from years of fighting on Traveler campgrounds, became even deadlier in the wrestling arena. "My old man had no problems," Gunn claims. "He destroyed everybody."

Robert was in business in Tampa in 1969 when his life took a turn that was even more turbulent than the wrestling circuit: love. By coincidence, he saw Jackie, a lovely dark-haired Traveler, leaving the Hawaiian Village, a Polynesian-themed resort near the airport. Instantly smitten, he made an audacious—and stupid—move, deliberately pushing his borrowed Pontiac convertible into the back of her vehicle to meet her. He was quickly escorted home to meet her father. "He didn't worry about the dented bumper," Robert laughs. "The old fella knew I was after his daughter." In the strict tribal world of the Travelers, defined by clan and religious affiliations, a Scottish Protestant like Robert marrying an Irish Catholic like Jackie was high treason—not as bad as marrying a non-Traveler, but still cause for rejection. "According to Traveler ways, my mom was never meant to marry my father," Gunn shares. "It's two different worlds, Catholic and Protestant, two different bloodlines." Despite their families' objections, Robert and Jackie were in love and wanted to be together, even if it meant complete alienation.

Robert, then twenty-six, and Jackie, twenty-four, married in 1969, less than six months after meeting. Although the union was not legally recognized (Robert never submitted the paperwork), the pair was happy and in love, and they soon relocated to Canada to continue working and traveling with the seasons. Pulling away from the wrestling circuit, Robert began living a more traditional life for his people, working odd jobs like painting, paving, and selling scrap while hoping to start a family. In Nova Scotia, he cut down trees with lumberjacks and fishermen. In the suburbs of Toronto, he painted barns and installed asphalt. He even proceeded into the United States, purchasing trailers in Indiana and driving them south to Monroe, Louisiana, to resell by the highway. "A gypsy guy I knew used to build 'em," Robert explains. "I'd pay three thousand for four of them and then sell them, making a couple grand a week—enough to have nice clothes."

Despite his best attempts, Robert could never give up his other hobbies, drinking and fighting. Robert would always go to the nearest pub after work, no matter where they were, and he would quickly get into trouble. In Nova Scotia, he fought local toughs in alleys for cash. In Toronto, he challenged Travelers in job disputes. In Monroe, Louisiana, he once provoked an all-out brawl in a pub by pouring beer into a saxophone player's instrument, resulting in a riot. Jackie would spend the night in the caravan, managing the money, cooking the meals, and healing Robert's bruises when he returned home before dawn. "Dad would take locals out back of the bars and make bets, punching the piss out of them," Gunn recalls. "Then he'd return to the KOA with bleeding knuckles, and my mother would inquire, 'What was the accident?Gunn laughs. "No accident—he punched the fuck out of three people."

Robert could never win a fight with his disapproving family members. In Niagara Falls, his Scottish Protestant neighbors may not have liked his Irish Catholic wife, Jackie, but they wouldn't dare to confront him over it. However, this would not be the case for her family. Soon after their wedding, Robert and his new bride came to her clan's campsite in Tampa for their first visit, and they instantly agreed to avoid any potential confrontations. Parking his caravan in the heart of their community, he turned on his loudspeakers and blared "The Old Orange Flute," a traditional song about a Protestant who marries a "Papist" woman and moves in with her family, only to have his flute refuse to play anything but British loyalist tunes like "Kick the Pope." The song was a blatant challenge to the campsite's hundred Irish Catholic families, an opening salvo about as subtle as pissing on a doorstep. Every Traveler there wished to dismember Robert. However, only one clan would receive the honors, and they arrived quickly.

Robert was sitting on his couch when he heard one of Jackie's cousins bang on the door and cry, "Get your fucking ass out now!" Prepared for the attack, Robert charged the door and kicked it open with both feet, knocking the man to the ground. "Dad kicks him in the chest, gets on top of him, and power-drives him with his right hands to the head, knocking his teeth out," Gunn recounts, having heard the story from uncles since childhood. "Then Dad jumps in the air, comes down, and breaks his leg. This occurred in under a minute. "Worst fucking mess you can imagine."

As the man lay unconscious, Robert began attacking his wife's other family members, with the men striking him and the women bashing him with tent poles, resulting in a massive melee that spread over the campsite. Finally, the cops arrived and discovered one of Jackie's relatives asleep, toothless, and with a broken leg. Robert was arrested and spent the following 30 days in jail. Jackie, furious at her husband for almost killing one of her family members, refused to post bail. "I knew, sooner or later, I was gonna have trouble," Robert recounts of the fight. "But I still felt awful about it since I had to live with it for so many years. I was married to Jackie. Do you understand what I mean?"

When Robert returned from jail, he appeared to have passed some type of test, and the Lindsay clan reluctantly accepted him into their fold. He started working for Jackie's father, Joe Lindsay, a huge 6'1" Irish Traveler who walked with a limp after being shot by an Indiana sheriff in 1920. In the 1980s, Robert would spend several weeks each winter traveling with Joe and his boys to campsites from Tampa to West Virginia to Ohio, paving roads by day and hitting bars by night. Once, in an Ohio saloon, Robert came into the bathroom to witness his father-in-law punching a man in the Adam's apple for some transgression, blood all over the toilet. Another time, in a dirt-floored salon in Kermit, West Virginia, Robert claims Joe was attempting to pick up a local coal miner's wife when her husband strolled in and pulled out a revolver. Robert stepped in, batting the husband's hand away and taking a gunshot through his foot. "I got a tetanus shot, and the doctor was some ol' guy chewing tobacco," Robert laughs. "West Virginia is not like being in the United States."

Gunn's grandfather, Joe, fought until he was eighty years old. Four young Travelers attempted to rob him, stabbing him several times before he fought them off. Despite winning the struggle, Joe shattered his fingers so severely that a doctor had to medically remove his gold saddle ring. When Gunn and his parents arrived in Florida and saw Joe in the hospital, he instructed them to empty his pockets, which still held a bit of an assailant's nose. "He told my dad to throw it in the garbage because he was worried about the cops," Gunn said. "He refused to take pain medication because he believed the doctor would steal his money. "The toughest man I've ever seen."

Gunn pauses. "I know all this fighting can sound sick and crazy to a normal person," he replies. "But if you look at our culture and way of thinking, winning a fight is what makes us proud. My father, and grandfathers, were men among men. The ground rocked beneath them as they moved. I wanted nothing more in life than to be like them.

CHAPTER 6
RAISED BY BLOOD

*G*unn's life was difficult from the start. His father may have earned the respect of his wife's family, but the truce was tense. As a result of his mixed Protestant and Catholic parentage, Gunn became an outcast, rejected by both sides of the family. "It's like being a half-breed," claims Jimmy Ruml. "He had no friends." When Gunn's wealthy relatives and uncles arrived, they insulted him and his parents. He was never allowed to attend children's parties at campers.

"I was invited to a birthday party, so my mother put a suit and tie on me," Gunn says. "I approach their RV trailer and present them a card; they give me a paper plate outdoors. They would not let me in." He stops. "That's heartbreaking."

Gunn, like his father and grandfather before him, rarely went to school, only attending lessons when the family was in Niagara Falls and then abruptly leaving. In second grade, a teacher accused Gunn of cheating on an exam, which he denied, and whacked his knuckles with a ruler. Gunn shoved the teacher, resulting in additional abuse. The next morning, Gunn's father arrived at school, grabbed the man by the tie, and threatened him. Gunn never returned to the classroom. He was 8 years old. "Mom tried to homeschool me, but it didn't take," he claims. "From then on, I was in the work truck with my father, out painting barn roofs, working hard and training." Gunn takes a look. "You see, I never had time to be a kid. I was a man before I became a man."

Gunn learned how to lay asphalt, paint homes, and work on building sites. As a boy, he would tie a rope around his waist and climb hundred-foot-tall grain silos, painting their steel hulls as his father shouted commands from below. Sometimes he would climb atop massive barns, assisting his father in spraying silver coating on sloped metal roofs while gazing out across the limitless Canadian prairie. "It seemed like we were on top of the world," Gunn says. "My dad would be silver, like the Tin Man. He would urge, 'Be brave, work hard.'" After that, Gunn and his father would strip down and wash the paint off their bodies while eating sandwiches provided by local farmers. For large works, Robert would employ Mohawk Indians from a nearby reservation to work for the day. One of Gunn's first memories is of Native Americans catching trout for meals, slicing open the silver bellies, inserting lemons, and then burying the fish in mud to bake over a riverside fire. Gunn, who had no friends, worked hard wherever they went in order to gain his father's approval. "Once, my dad gave me fifty dollars for a day's pay, saying, 'Good boy, I'm proud of you,'" Gunn remembers. "I was a little boy but quite proud of myself. "I was helping him."

Despite his best attempts, Gunn's childhood remained difficult. His parents would sometimes have severe conflicts, and Robert would disappear for days at a time. After his father left, Gunn, a young kid, put a phone book in the driver's seat of the family work truck and drove about town looking for work to support his mother. "They had a really bad argument and separated," Gunn remembers. "So, I had to be a man. We sometimes had to put water on our cereal because we didn't have any milk. "It was a difficult time."

Even when Robert stayed, finances were tight. Some of his family in Niagara Falls did well in construction, even owning their own asphalt businesses, but they never helped Robert, most likely because of his marriage to Jackie. "I had a lot of family that made good money in construction," Gunn tells me. "Very regular. Kids wore good outfits. But they refused to take us with them. Gunn grew up impoverished and socially isolated. He admired boxers, but they discouraged him from fighting. He attempted to befriend cousins, but they would take him to restaurants and then mock him for not being able to afford food. Robert would occasionally protect his son, once confronting two family members who had mocked Gunn for being poor. However, Gunn was largely left to fend for himself. "They treated me like dog shit," he said of his extended family. "They really damaged my heart. I would be so mortified that I would simply go mute. There were only a few people who treated me well as a child."

Gunn could only find one source of solace, which he poured his heart and soul into: fighting. "I took the loneliness and turned it into creative things in my mind by mimicking fight moves," he explains. "It upset me that I didn't have the same things as other youngsters. But I knew I'd have to go grab that item. I would have to be a hustler. "No one was giving me anything."

Gunn aspired to be a world champion boxer since he was a child. He admired Travelers like the Hilton brothers, five Montreal siblings who used their fists to escape the camps and become wealthy and renowned as professional boxers in Canada. "The fighting Hiltons were my heroes," he jokes. "They were Travelers, and they were so popular that they looked like the boys on the Wheaties box. They were fucking superheroes." With little schooling or prospects, Gunn turned to combat as his only option for a better life, quickly creating a strategy. He would win an Olympic medal and a world crown, kicking off his own extraordinary career. "I wanted to be a world champion," Gunn explains. "I wanted to prove to everyone of my family members who told me I'd never have anything. "Fighting was all I had."

Gunn first started brawling in the trailer parks. Each year, as the weather warmed, Robert would hook the family's dilapidated caravan to his truck and drive west through the plains, the Rockies, and occasionally all the way to the Pacific Northwest, knocking on farmers' doors seeking employment and sleeping together in parks on the outskirts of towns. "It was a little tiny RV trailer, no heat or electricity," Gunn tells me. "I'd walk to a water faucet and brush my teeth and wash myself outside." During the summer, the campgrounds were teeming with Scottish, Irish, and English travelers from all over North America, all on the road and looking for work. Far from the romanticized campfire idylls of fantasy, these parks were battle zones—desolate, hazardous, trash-strewn fields of broken glass populated by squatters and feral dogs.

"They were all gravel, no grass," Ruml explains. "Working-class types who disliked strangers." It was a difficult life, especially for children." The locals disliked the Travelers, and they fought among themselves along clan lines. Gunn was nearly kidnapped as a child by a child molester, but his grandfather stepped in at the last minute, pummeling the offender and phoning the cops.

The Gunns would occasionally journey with other Scottish Traveler families, exchanging employment suggestions and pooling money, forming alliances to defend themselves in the campgrounds. Most of the time, however, the family managed to exist on their own. And, as Gunn quickly learned from his mother, vulnerability was not an option.

Jacqueline Gunn was a stunning brunette, a loving mother and wife, and possibly the toughest member of the family. "She was a lioness," Ruml says. As an Irish Catholic Traveler who had abandoned her people for Robert and moved north to live with his openly hostile Scottish Protestant clan, she had to fight every day merely to raise her family.

"A lot of people weren't nice to her," Gunn claims. "They'd ask my father, 'Why did you marry an Irish girl, a Papist? "You should not have done that."

Jackie would try to make amends by inviting her husband's family into their house. "One time, my father's cousins and uncles came and visited in their big shiny cars and trucks, the smell of cologne off them," Gunn shares. "My poor mother, she's a proud gypsy woman, but we weren't doing well, and it showed. But she was pleasant and remarked to one of the little guys, 'Oh, you're so handsome; what a lovely sweater. We should purchase one for Bobby. So, where did you acquire it?And the man replied, 'Darling, you couldn't afford it. "Take him to Goodwill and get him something." Gunn pauses. "After they left, my mother began to cry." She glanced at me and whispered, 'Don't forget this day for the rest of your life. "You'll have it all."

Jackie remained sober despite Robert's occasional weeks-long drinking binges. She went to mass, told her small son Old Testament stories about Israelites defeating Philistines, and glared down at every single son of a bitch that threatened her family. "She could be sweet, but God help the person that came after her little boy," according to Ruml. "Man or woman—she wasn't afraid of anybody."

As a boy, Gunn recalls his mother frequently fighting in the campgrounds. "Today, the Traveler girls do not fight," Gunn states. "But my mother wouldn't think twice. She'd put her hair in a bandanna, Vaseline on her face, and punch your fucking head off." In a faded family portrait of his mother that Gunn maintains, Jackie is looking passionately at the camera, her brown eyes hard, her hair in a towering beehive, and her hands holding up her infant son's fists in a battle posture. She once knocked her own spouse unconscious during a heated argument. "She exclaimed, 'Come on, you bitch!"And knocked my dad back three feet," Gunn claims. "The old girl was game."

In the early 1980s, while the Gunn family was camping in rural Ontario, an older English Traveler adolescent began a fight with Gunn, who was then approximately eight years old. Despite the age and size gap, Gunn managed to take the kid to the ground and was hitting him until the boy's mother intervened, slapped Gunn across the face and sent him home. After seeing her son's welt, Jackie marched to the English Travelers' trailer and confronted the mother, who stepped outside with her three sisters. When she realized she was outnumbered, Jackie went home, wrapped two rolls of pennies in two of her husband's work socks, clasped the money in her fists, and returned to the English Travelers' caravan. Jackie got to work quickly after calling the sisters outside. "She fucking leveled 'em," Gunn claims. "Whack! I mean, they started running. I recall the last one she beat, the boy's mother, the fucking sock ripped, and coins scattered everywhere. Mom grabbed her by the hair, yanked off her blouse, and smacked the fuck out of her. 'Stop it!'I yelled. Oh, God, she was tough!"

Sometimes the entire Gunn family fought together. Gunn was ten years old and camping in the wild forests of northern Saskatchewan when three young English Traveler brothers grabbed him, destroying his pistol and assaulting him with it. "They whacked me, punched me, jumped on me, kicked me, and laughed at me," Gunn told me. "I got up, went home, and Mom fixed me a lunch. She asked, "What happened to you?"'Nothing, nothing, nothing.' 'Where's your gun?'It's broken.' 'What do you mean by that?'" Enraged, Jackie took Gunn's hand, rushed straight to the English Travelers' trailer, located the teens' mother, and confronted her. "She said, 'Now, listen here, you dirty cockney bastard, your boys beat my wee boy,'" Gunn recollects. "'Come out here and apologize.' The woman said, 'Nah, he was looking for it.' So my mom grabbed her right out of the trailer and began punching the fucking head off her." When one of the English Traveler kids stepped in and swung at Jackie, she flung him to the ground. When Gunn saw his mother in distress, he grabbed a bat and hit the teenager in the leg. With a gathering forming, Jackie drew her kid back. "As we were walking away, Mom yelled, 'Wait till my husband gets home,'" Gunn told me.

At seven, Robert returned to the park, heard the story, saw his son's bruises, and simply answered, "All right." He marched to the English

Travelers' trailer, dragged the father outside, and began pounding him. Then, when the teenage sons appeared, he leveled them as well. "He beat the fuck out of all of them," Gunn claims. "My mom was standing right there." The Gunns eventually returned home, but the fight was far from done. The English Traveler father, wielding a shotgun, barged into the Gunns' caravan in the middle of the night. Robert crept into his work vehicle, gunned the engine, and slammed the English Traveler family's trailer with his extended-cab dually. My father roared, 'You cocksuckers, now we're going to fucking war!"Gunn recalls. The English Travelers, along with the rest of their clan, abandoned the place rather than continue the feud. Soon, the cops arrived. Robert said that his clutch had become stuck and that he had accidently drove into the trailer, assuring them that he would resolve the situation with the family when they returned. "He squared the whole thing away," Gunn says. "And then went back to work the next morning."

Robert was the family's final line of defense, and only Jackie could calm him down when he became enraged. Gunn would frequently wake up in the mornings to find his mother spraying blood off the concrete slab next to their trailer—the residue of his father's brawls from the night before, caked and crusted on the asphalt. "I remember bloody handprints on the side of our RV trailer," he tells me. "Mom outside the next day washing it off."

In the early 1980s, the family was eating supper on a campsite in North Bay, Ontario, when they were startled by a guy knocking on their door—a Traveler who had come to confront Robert about a job-related issue. Robert walked out, leaving his soup on the table, and immediately began fighting the man, exchanging punches until he threw him to the ground and straddled him. "Instead of choking him, my father put his hands in his mouth, took his two fingers on each side of his cheeks, and started ripping," Gunn tells me. "My mother came out screaming, 'Stop it, you're going to kill him!'""The man was laying on the ground, blood flowing out of him, and Dad just stood up and walked away." In the trailer, Robert returned to his seat at the table. "He's all blood," Gunn explains. "So he combs his hair, applies aftershave, and returns to his soup. Twenty minutes later, the old guy says, "Is he gone yet?"'Mom is just looking at him. She knew the man had come seeking it and that my father had to go fight him. She was an authentic gypsy woman. But she intervened because she knew he was about to kill him." Gunn pauses. "I'll never forget the poor bastard outside, who eventually got up and drove away, bleeding all over his truck, while my father watched TV. Dad was a hard fucking guy."

Feuds between Traveler families may persist for years, passed down through generations like an inheritance, with the origins long forgotten but the hate still present. One of Gunn's first memories is of his father standing in a telephone booth, relaying news of a win over another Traveler to his grandparents. The man Robert had defeated was the son of a man his own father had fought and defeated decades earlier, marking the latest victory in a generations-long battle between the clans. "My grandmother got on the phone and asked, 'Did your father give it to him well?"'Gunn recalls. "'Oh, absolutely, unbelievable, Grannie.' 'Well done. All right, my dear. "We love you." Gunn pauses. "It's unreal, my family."

Gunn's upbringing was a collage of Traveler camping brawls, an unending struggle for survival. But there was one fight that stood out for its severity, one in which he began to establish his own reputation among his people, and it took place, of all places, at Disney World. For visitors, the Magic Kingdom is a unique place. The spired castles, plush dolls, and carnival rides provide a neutral ground, a theme-park Switzerland where warring tribes can coexist peacefully. Gunn took a day off from work as a teenager in Tampa to visit the park with thirty other young Travelers. He spent the day roaming the grounds and enjoying the rides, dressed in a blue suit and leather shoes, until the trouble began late in the afternoon, when he and the other youths returned to the parking lot. There, among the sun-beaten automobiles, was a 6'2" 200-pound Irish Traveler in his early twenties—an older, more well-known brawler who was shirtless and coated with Vaseline. "It was even all through his hair," Gunn says. The man approached Gunn—then a rising fighter in his own right—and challenged him. Gunn declined. Because of his mixed origins, he had never been fully accepted by his people. However, without them, he had no tribe to call his own. "I don't want to fight you, pal," Gunn explained.

Ignoring him, the Irishman charged. Gunn delivered two jabs before throwing him face first into the side of a pickup truck. The bleeding man rose up and charged at Gunn, who smacked him with a straight right hand, knocking him on the asphalt. Then something unusual occurred. The Irishman started crying, advancing as if to hug Gunn about the waist—and sinking his teeth into Gunn's upper leg. "He was trying to bite my dick off," Gunn explains. "I buried my hand in his curly hair, yanked back his head, and chewed the top of his ear off. I delivered two left hooks—bang, bang!—and his teeth fell out like Chiclets, and he fell to the ground." The Irishman's family wrapped him in painter's drop cloth and drove him to the hospital. Gunn, his suit stained and ripped, returned home. He was about to leave the Traveler battlegrounds forever.

"It was a hard, lonely life, the good ol' Traveler country," Gunn elaborates. "It wasn't right and it wasn't wrong—but it wasn't normal."

CHAPTER 7
WARRIORS OF FAITH

*A*s a child, Gunn struggled for the same reasons he does now: money, family, and religion. "Jesus Christ and his disciples were warriors," Gunn explains. "These were rugged, strong men who went to war and endured abuse. If we do not have a divine foundation as humans, we shall become animals. Fighting has been around since Biblical times.

Surprisingly, Gunn and the other Travelers of North America continue to live by the same beliefs as their wagon-roaming forefathers in the nineteenth century. However, unlike their modern British counterparts, who's fighting and habits have been depicted in countless documentaries, TV series, novels, and films—most famously as Brad Pitt's mumbling knuckler in Snatch—the Travelers of North America are completely unknown. They are ghosts, a mythological civilization, and a mystery tribe that avoids all outsiders. "We haven't done any research on them here," says George Gmelch, cultural anthropology professor at the University of San Francisco who specializes in Travelers of Ireland. "There just isn't very much."

This is by design. In seven years of reporting, I've yet to meet Gunn's wife, Rose, or see inside their apartment. Gunn has never let me record his people's secret language. "My wife doesn't want to talk, because she doesn't want to be persecuted by other Travelers for speaking to outsiders," Gunn declares. "If I wasn't in the public eye, I wouldn't be able to associate with country people. "I'd be rejected."

Only one man, Catholic priest John Stygles of Memphis, has gained access to their closed-off culture. And what he's discovered is incredible: an underground society that upholds Old World customs like arranged marriages, wandering trades, mystical religion, and bare-knuckle combat in the heart of twenty-first-century America. "They don't speak to outsiders, because they've been criticized and attacked," Stygles shares. "The joke is, they call their language Cant because 'You can't understand us.'"

Gunn's paternal family were traveling from Scotland to Canada around the turn of the century, as his mother's folks, the Lindsays, were arriving in the United States. According to Irish Traveler legend and Stygles' study, the first eight families to describe their trades as "tinker" in America arrived in New York with a larger wave of European immigrants in the mid-nineteenth century. Working as horse and mule traders, these Travelers settled mostly in livestock auction hubs throughout the south, where the three largest groups of descendants still live in close-knit enclaves of double-wide trailers and subdivisions—the "Mississippi Travelers" in the Memphis area; the "Georgia Travelers" just across the state line in Murphy Village, South Carolina; and the "Texas Travelers" in Fort Worth. 2 Smaller Traveler communities can also be found throughout the United States, from Wilmington, Delaware, to St. Augustine, Florida, to Dayton, Ohio, to Los Angeles.

The first US Travelers, known as "Irish horse traders," "pedlars," or "the walking people," were shockingly wealthy, according to nineteenth- and twentieth-century periodicals. They were savvy traders who purchased emaciated mules and horses, nursed them back to health, and then sold them for a profit. They also purchased investment properties across the country, with the land serving as camping grounds during their travels. According to media reporting in the south between 1901 and 1908, the "straightforward, hardworking. ..studiously law-abiding clans roved in groups of fifty in carts resembling "circus wagons," regularly attending church with their "neatly dressed" children. Every spring, the Travelers would convene to mingle and to bury their dead in appointed plots in

Atlanta and Nashville, the women wearing "jeweled crucifixes and rosaries" for the communal wakes, the men flashing diamond rings. "Wandering homeless through the south, yet doing an annual cash business of hundreds of thousands of dollars; living in tents like gypsy nomads yet the owners of many city lots and valuable town property," states a newspaper in Springfield, Illinois, in 1913. "Such is the strange life of the Irish clan." 5

Today, an estimated ten thousand Travelers live in the United States, mostly working in construction and continuing to live a semi-nomadic life, traveling for work nine months of the year and roosting in the winter. Despite being undocumented by the US Census Bureau, they self-identify as an ethnic group based on descent. They are suspicious of Giorgio, marry almost exclusively within their tribe, expel those who leave, and usually remove their children from school by the eighth grade to prevent them from assimilation into mainstream culture. "University will ruin them," Jimmy Ruml warns. "Traveling provides freedom. Once you quit, they have you."

Outsiders have a poor reputation, which gives travelers cause to be afraid of them. As Gunn will admit, it is occasionally justified. Google "Irish Travelers" and you'll find a slew of media clippings about small scams. Travelers have been known to target neighborhoods and the elderly, offering to fix roofs, paint houses, or resurface driveways, only to use thin mixtures that quickly wear away. Or they'll claim to be traveling salesmen, selling shoddy equipment or tools at a premium price, then charging the customers an exorbitant rate to fix them. Errant Travelers have even popped up in murder investigations, and, in a high-profile case in 2014, were on the front end.

Gunn is keen to point out that the Travelers' reputation is inflated. "Out of a hundred Travelers, ninety-five have done good for themselves in life," he informs me. "Did you know that my people have recently repaved the White House Drive?" Yes, as Gunn would confirm, there are cliques of Travelers who engage in systematic fraud. But the concept that they, as a people, are running a statewide criminal network to defraud other Americans is absurd, if not openly bigoted. Stygles agrees. "They're good people," he says. "Most Irish Travelers simply work really hard in a field about which many people complain—home repairs and the like. They aren't who you believe they are. "You cannot stereotype them."

For Gunn, like with most US travelers, the three simple values of family, faith, and battling are everything. Lineages are learned at birth in Traveler culture. The elderly are cared for. Children grow up surrounded by parents, aunts, uncles, and cousins. The family structures are strict from the nineteenth century, with men doing the job and women tending the home. Work, whether constant, arduous, or physical, begins at an early age. Corporate day jobs are unheard of. In fact, they are looked down upon. Working for a Gorgio is considered humiliating. Instead, after leaving school at the age of fifteen, boys generally apprentice with their fathers, learning a skill and living at home until they can generate an income and, as a result, marry. The Travelers are not as reclusive as the Amish—they work with Gorgio when necessary, have cell phones, and watch TV—but they also do not invite visitors back to the trailer park. "It's just easier to hang out with other travelers," Bobby Jr. explains. "You don't have to explain so much."

Gunn's voice is perhaps the most telling sign of his outsider status. Travelers, an isolated society with a hidden language, are known for their unique accents. In 2012, for his role as the villain Bane in The Dark Knight Rises, actor Tom Hardy based his voice on champion bare-knuckle fighter Bartley Gorman, knowing that the Traveler's accent would heighten his character's mystery. The "accent" was highly specific. ..In a 2012 interview, Hardy admitted to having a Gypsy accent. "That's why it was difficult to understand." In his 1946 novel Nightmare Alley, author William Lindsay Gresham portrays the placeless accents of American circus workers, who are frequently thrown in with travelers. "[Their speech] was a composite of all the sprawling regions of the country," Gresham writes in her book. "A language that seemed Southern to Southerners and Western to Westerners. It was the talk of the land. .."A soothing, illiterate, and earthy language."

Gunn, like the other Travelers, has an odd voice. His accent and speech are simultaneously placeless and ageless, with a Scottish-Canadian lilt mixed with a 1940s street-tough lexicon that sounds like he just emerged from a bunker after decades of isolation from mainstream society. He refers to boxers as "pals," female tollbooth operators as "darlings" or "my angels," and ends texts with "my brother." His favorite phrase is "fair play to you," which is traveler slang for best wishes on a clean fight. He and his children frequently forsake English entirely, lowering their voices and slipping in and out of Cant, the Travelers' secret language, in front of Gorgio and Musker, the latter being their term for police. "It's our own code."

However, while Gunn follows many long-held family traditions, he, like other modern Travelers, has made some modern concessions. As a northern Traveler, he rejects arranged marriage—"it's a redneck thing"—and has abandoned the nomadic encampments of his youth to raise his family in an apartment. He refuses to let his son fight bare-knuckle. And his daughter, Charlene, will not marry at the age of sixteen. "She's my little girl," he says. "Not until eighteen or twenty."

Gunn, on the other hand, continues to follow some traditions. He took Bobby Jr. out of school after seventh grade and began homeschooling him while simultaneously bringing him into the asphalt company. Despite working long hours to pay for Charlene's private school education, Gunn believes she will not attend classes at her current school beyond fifth grade. "She has all her little friends right now, but they will start to drift apart," he jokes. "If a Traveler girl goes to school with country people, she might not marry a Traveler boy." Charlene will most likely spend her days studying how to manage the family money, which is a customary duty for women in the Traveler household.

When I'm alone with Bobby Jr., I ask him whether he ever wanted to be a part of the outside world or if he feels like he's missing out. "Nah," he says. "You've seen the film 300, correct? Their culture revolved around training, fighting, and making war. People questioned it, yet they had the best military in the world. For travelers, it's simply our way. We were born to do this."

Ultimately, Gunn will not compromise on the two most important aspects of Traveler heritage: faith and fighting. Whether Catholic or Protestant, Travelers embrace a devout blend of Christianity and Irish Druidism, a nearly medieval belief system in which God's actual word is revered and saints and demons coexist. For many, the Bible is the only book they will ever read. "It's very much an Old World outlook," Stygles explains. "You'd see the same thing on the north end of Boston, with old Italian widows wearing black and playing with their rosary beads. The travelers think that God will protect them. It's a traditional way of doing things." Some Travelers believe they are the descendants of Cain, who was banished by God in the Old Testament for killing Abel—"a fugitive and a vagabond shall thou be in the earth." Others say they hail from the blacksmith who forged the nails for Jesus' cross, his progeny forever flung to the wild. Traveler men carry rosaries, wear decade rings with bumps on the shank for counting prayers, and hang crosses from their rearview mirrors.

Gunn does not drink, which is remarkable because alcohol and tobacco are not prohibited. "That's just us," Gunn adds, indicating to Bobby Jr. "Travelers love to drink—the beer factory couldn't fill them."

Shunning is perhaps the most biblical characteristic of Traveler civilization. When a Traveler breaks a tribe rule, he must go church and request forgiveness as penance, or the clan will reject him. "If you go back to the biblical times, it was a shame-or-honor society," according to Stygles. "Well, that's how it works in this community too." At one point, Gunn narrates a story of a Traveler who defrauded him of money. Gunn might have easily beaten the man, but it would have been an unjust fight. Instead, he humiliated him in the most degrading manner conceivable. Gunn approached the man while he was enjoying dinner with his family in his home, summoned him outside to fight and settle the dispute, and then stood over him as he refused to move, forcing him to bear the mark of a coward. "He never even looked at me," Gunn explains. "And his children will never look at him the same way again."

Every night before going to bed, Gunn lies entirely prostrate on the floor, praying for the strength of his faith and the safety of his family from sin. When he's not exercising at Ike's, he works out with chain-smoking Polish priests at a Polish gym in Jersey City, listening to their stories about modern-day exorcisms in rural towns. They talk of odd instances in which eighty-pound females snap the necks of horses and speak in languages, as well as the week-long process of banishing the "roughy"—Travelers won't even mention the devil's name aloud—from their hearts. "If you don't believe it," said Gunn, "then you can get taken out."

Only once has Gunn lost faith. He stopped attending church in the summer of 1999, while traveling through the Midwest with his family, knocking on doors to drum up paving jobs, and money was tight at every step. "I just wasn't walking with God," he adds.

Gunn awoke one night in a Candlewood Suites in Ohio to intense chest pressure, as if a weight was smothering him. He looked up. He claims that a pale face with crimson eyes and a black body hovered above him, lingering before disappearing into the darkness. Gunn lay motionless, shaking. He looked at the bedside clock, which read 3:16. He dashed to the floor cot, checked on Bobby Jr., who was just two years old at the time, and got back into bed 10 minutes later. The clock was still showing 3:16. Gunn cried. His wife, Rose, inquired as to what was wrong. "It was a message," Gunn explains. "John 3:16: For God so loved the world that he gave his one and only son."

Violence is a natural part of life for Travelers who have grown up with the Old Testament and its eye-for-an-eye philosophy. Pit bulls are unleashed on feral pigs in Florida wetlands, hunting and slashing the 400-pound creatures through the armpits with six-inch blades. In northern Oklahoma, quarter horses are raced in dried-up riverbeds in illegal events near Indian reservations, while gamblers and drinkers congregate on the barren plains. They hunt gear at night in the bayous of Gulf Coast Texas with compound bows from flat-bottom boats, spotlighting the prehistoric-looking fish before impaling them with double-barbed carbon-shaft arrows.

Fighting, however, is the most revered and devoutly practiced blood sport. Gunn leads an ascetic lifestyle, considering his body as a temple and remaining healthy because, as scripture indicates, adversity is to be expected—and overcome only with power. "My mother used to read the Bible to me at night," he jokes. "Jesus Christ was not the destitute, scrawny guy shown on the crucifixion. He was a gruff man, a carpenter who worked with enormous timbers and stones. When he turned over the marble tables in that marketplace, they were estimated to weigh one hundred pounds. And he endured a battering that no one else did. Fighting has always been a part of humanity. I believe it is not a sin if you have no hatred for the man. But if you are a bully, you are not of God. Then you pay the price."

CHAPTER 8
THROUGH PAIN AND GRIEF

*F*or Gunn, the fight was about vengeance. In August, he lost his first professional boxing fight against García in a Top Rank battle in Las Vegas due to a fractured right arm that cracked in two in the second round. "I got punched in the arm, and the bone was nearly sticking out of the skin," Gunn said. "The referee exclaimed, 'Oh my God!' and ended the fight." Seven months later, famed trainer Johnny Tocco, who helped shape everyone from Sonny Liston to Mike Tyson in a gym next to a Las Vegas tire-repair shop, helped set up a rematch. Gunn saw the fight as a critical step toward redeeming his loss and, perhaps, finally proving to promoter Don King's camp that he was ready for the big time. Gunn was just eighteen years old, but he had been boxing professionally for three years. "I couldn't get the proper respect that I really wanted," according to him. "I was just a sparring partner for all the top guys in the world."

Kenny "The Emerald City Assassin" Ellis, a former professional middleweight and Gunn's sparring partner, recounts his friend's struggles. "Bobby had the face of a choirboy and the left hook of a hell boy," Ellis says. "He worked alongside Don King. We arrived in town full of optimism and left in broken spirits, our pants tied with rope."

Mike Hopper, a sixty-year-old professional boxing trainer from Memphis who handled Gunn's corner in the 1990s, attributes Gunn's inability to break through to management. "Back then, Gunn was a smaller guy, a middleweight, a gaudy-style fighter, a crowd pleaser," Hopper tells me. "If he had good people around him at the time, he could have gone on to do what he needed to do in the boxing world. But sometimes you get a bad-apple manager who isn't looking out for your best interests—he's looking out for his own."

Gunn had been promised stardom, but by the time he reached Tijuana, he was beginning to doubt everything. Despite his hard work, talent, and assurances from promoter Carl King (the stepson of Don King, who was widely said to have truly run the show), Gunn had been given fights only in dead-end outposts like Phoenix, Juárez, and Baja California. For the most part, he had been used as a sparring partner, that most dispensable of underlings, who fights the A-list roster to keep them in shape, sacrificing his own health to h Gunn lost his first bout against García due to a hairline fracture sustained during a practice session with Don King's middleweight world champion Mike McCallum three days prior. Gunn's team did not want to postpone the fight, so he entered the ring with a broken arm, eventually breaking the fracture clean during his encounter. "They didn't want to lose money on the fight," Gunn claims. "So they shot me with something like Novocain and sent me out." Seven months later in Tijuana, Gunn, restored to health, dropped García in minutes. "I did what I shoulda done the first time," he says.

Perhaps García, a southern California native, was a local favorite. Perhaps the audience had wagered against the gringo. Perhaps they were just inebriated and furious that the fight had ended so quickly. Whatever the cause, they decided to take it out on the perpetrator. The place erupted.

Gunn just had time to remove one glove before the chain-link dressing room was kicked down. Still in his trunks, he slipped by a back door, leaped into the back of a waiting car, and was led by police across the border.

The driver, an old boxer who works for Johnny Tocco, lit a joint and turned on the radio. Marijuana smoke and music filled the Lincoln Continental as he drove them north into the desert, with Gunn looking out the window. Gunn had won the battle, but the circumstances were horrible. Rubbing his knuckles, he reflected on his future with the King, how he could possibly make it as a fighter with a damaged arm, and how he would continue to support his mother. He felt far from attaining the dreams of his wild childhood.

History is riddled with instances of travelers going bare-knuckle only to flare out in dramatic fashion later. In the eighteenth century, Benjamin Boswell, a highway robber and boxer, drew large crowds to London before quitting the sport and likely returning to a life of crime. In England in the 1970s, "Gypsy Johnny" Frankham, a Romany Gypsy who chain-smoked, drank, and gambled away his winnings, managed to win the British title before fading out and being convicted of fraud. In Montreal in the 1980s, five Scottish Traveler brothers known as the "fighting Hiltons" grew up sha These included rape, discharging a revolver in a hotel lobby, and robbing a Dunkin' Donuts for $160. In 2012, Irish Traveler John Joe Nevin earned a silver medal at the Olympics, only to have both legs crushed shortly thereafter by a family member with a golf club. The attack caused his right tibia to protrude from the skin, and his career quickly slipped into an alcohol-soaked slump.

Of all Traveler pro boxers, none would fall as spectacularly as Tyson Fury, a 6'9" slugger who won the world heavyweight championship belt in 2015—a feat unmatched by any Traveler in history—only to firebomb his career in a cocaine-fueled collapse that stripped him of his titles and nearly killed him.

Fury, who is descended from a long line of bare-knuckle boxers, was raised in a trailer in Manchester, England. His father, "Gypsy" John, was a bare-knuckle champion who was sentenced to eleven years in prison for gouging out an opponent's eye in a street brawl. His uncle, Pete, was a street fighter who rose to become a crime boss in Manchester in the 1980s, importing amphetamines from Belgium and distributing them across northwest England. Pete was sentenced to ten years in prison in 1995, following a life filled with Ferraris and turf battles. Following his release in 2008, he was accused of money laundering. "I was regarded as dangerous, so I was locked up with

IRA members and lifers," he stated in 2013. "I found fighting a release." When Tyson's father, John, was imprisoned for street fighting, Pete, who had served his sentence, took over Tyson's training. The former crime leader then helped his nephew to a shock victory over Wladimir Klitschko in 2015, which earned Fury the WBA (Super), IBF, WBO, IBO, and Ring magazine heavyweight titles. "Nothing can ever, ever mean more to my family, my history of people, than winning those titles," he says. "We are bare-knuckle champions, boxing champions—all that matters to us is fighting."

From the moment he won the world title, when he grabbed the mic, turned away from the stone-face Ukrainian, thanked God, and then, weeping, belted out Aerosmith's "I Don't Want to Miss a Thing" to his wife, Paris, it was clear that Fury would be no ordinary world champion. Within weeks, the Gypsy Kings sexist, homophobic, and downright bizarre remarks—at one point, he asserted that the apocalypse was nigh and Klitschko was a devil worshiper—led to a petition to remove

Nothing compared to the bombshell that broke in September 2016, when ESPN reported that Fury had failed a cocaine test. In lieu of an official statement, the world heavyweight champion responded to the allegations by taking to Twitter, where he posted a series of strange tweets, including a Photoshopped image of himself sitting behind a Scarface-worthy mountain of coke, an announcement of his retirement, and then an immediate retraction of the announcement, all of which made global headlines. In the end, he admitted to the allegations, lost all of his titles, and was hospitalized for suicidal bipolar disorder, stating that constant prejudiced comments online had driven him over the brink. "I used to love boxing as a kid and always thought once I got to the top, everything would change," Fury added, alluding to his alleged struggles with depression and racism. "But deep down, I knew it never would."

Fury, on the other hand, would soon make a storybook recovery, becoming the world's lineal and WBC heavyweight champion—and serving as a beacon of hope for Travelers like Gunn.

Bobby Gunn was resolved to overcome the Traveler curse and become a world champion pro boxer without losing his titles or his sanity. As a young man, he appeared ready to do so. In 1988, at age fifteen, he was a rising amateur star who had trained with the Gatti brothers in Jersey City, exhibited for famed trainer Slim Robinson in Philadelphia, and even flown to Texas to spar for an oil heiress, Josephine Abercrombie, in her fledgling (and ultimately doomed) Houston Boxing Association. Living in shabby motels in Niagara Falls, Gunn could have signed with any number of promoters but ultimately decided to go with the top name in the world: Don K According to Gunn and his father, King, a wild-haired boxing star who has supported everyone from Muhammad Ali to Oscar De La Hoya to Mike Tyson, offered Gunn a non contract job as a sparring partner—a low-level role for entry-level boxers to prepare them for prime time. "Bobby was hanging out with Don King's crew, sparring with all the big names," Hopper tells me. "He was a youngster taking on the big-timers." Gunn would earn $500 every week, enough to cover the family expenditures and save for a surgery for his mother, who had lately fallen seriously ill. Gunn agreed to the terms, excited about the opportunity to work with King. "I was the youngest fighter they had," he recalls. According to his childhood friend, Mike Normile, "They threw him to the wolves." (King did not answer many interview requests.)

Without his mother, Gunn may never have been a professional fighter. The year before he began fighting for King, Jackie had walked out of a coffee shop at night and tripped on a piece of black ice, shattering her head on the sidewalk and lying unconscious until a worker discovered her frozen body attached to the ice. "Her hip was busted," Gunn explains. "Twisted behind her back." In the ER, doctors conducted hip surgery and administered a blood transfusion.

A year later, she stated that she was not feeling well. After undergoing blood testing, Jackie discovered that she had been infected with hepatitis C, which was already devouring her liver and would kill her within months. Then she received even worse news. "The doctor said, 'We can't even give you a liver transplant, because your citizenship ain't right,'" Gunn remembers. Jackie and Robert had never obtained legal documentation for their unauthorized Traveler marriage, therefore as an American citizen, she was ineligible for Canada's health care. "What did we have to do?" Gunn asks. "Go to America."

In 1988, the Gunns relocated to Las Vegas, the world's fight capital, so Gunn could earn enough money in the ring to cover Jackie's hospital bills. While making the rounds with his father and meeting promoters, Gunn lied about his age, claiming to be eighteen, the legal minimum age to fight professionally in Nevada. The family resided in a run-down apartment on Koval Lane, just off the Strip, and Jackie remained uninsured. Her only option was to undergo a liver transplant, which would cost at least $23,000 if not covered by insurance. Overwhelmed by his wife's illness and their financial situation, Robert fell into a deep melancholy, drinking for days on end and doing nothing except focusing on a last-ditch effort to preserve his family's fortunes—selling Bobby as a superstar fighter. "The best trainers in the world said Bobby could hit three times as hard as any man," Bob recalls. "He did it all, seen it all."

Robert made the rounds, touting his son as the next Ali, meeting potential managers and promoters in gyms and hotel suites along the Strip, even sitting down with actor Gene Hackman, who had just made the boxing film Split Decisions and loved the sport, racing cars with Panamanian lightweight champion Alexis Argüello and helping start a foundation for impoverished former fighters. "He wanted a piece of me," Gunn recalls. "He owned a portion of the Ruelas brothers. Gene Hackman was a man's man. I liked him." Out of all his meetings, Robert was most struck by Don King, the world's most famous and ruthless promoter. At the time, King was a powerful dictator with Troll Doll hair, having pitted Muhammad Ali against George Foreman in the 1974 "Rumble in the Jungle" in Zaire and now overseeing boxers such as Julio César Chávez and Mike Tyson. His mastery of boxing was absolute. King operated as a promoter, while his stepson, Carl King, served as manager for all of their boxers, getting at least 33% of the purses. Although this was frequently mentioned as a conflict of interest—managers are meant to ensure that their fighters are treated properly by promoters—the arrangement was not unlawful.

In fact, King was frequently able to manage both fighters in the same fight, ensuring that he would win regardless of the result. "In this corner, a Don King fighter," wrote Michael Katz of the New York Times in 1983. "In that corner there's a Don King warrior. Frequently, they are administered by Carl, the promoter's adopted son. ..This regular matchup is an entrance to monopoly for an expanding number of furious and resentful competitors.

Gunn found solace in his friendships with his fellow low-level boxers, fringe contenders like Mike "the Bounty" Hunter, a LA fighter who was later shot dead by police on Sunset Boulevard in 2005, and Ellis, a Seattle middleweight who now works as a caregiver for special-needs people in Phoenix. "We were both green as pool tables," Ellis recalls, laughing. "Bobby was pretty much the only white guy, but he's not white. He was a nomad and knew some of the difficulties we faced. Bobby was one of us." Gunn would frequently bring combatants back to his family's apartment, where his mother would get up for a few hours to cook Irish stew while his father sat in the background, the stench of alcohol wafting off him like a fog. "His mom was one of God's hand picked angels," Ellis says. "But his dad was a gritty, tough old man—Papa didn't make any mess."

After years of sparring, Gunn finally saved the $23,000 required for his mother's surgery. The family located a clinic in Pittsburgh. Gunn claims he stepped into a room, met a hospital representative sitting next to a lawyer, and handed them the total amount in cash. "These are professional cons," Gunn says. "The medical profession is all about making money."

While waiting for the operation, Gunn went to work the bags in a boxing club in Pittsburgh's tough neighborhood, where he received an offer that would forever change his life. After the session, the manager approached him and asked if he wanted to make some money. "The guy said, 'There's an underground bare-knuckle fight happening here,'" Gunn remembers. "Do you want in?'" The stakes were high—$3,000. Gunn didn't have the money because he had spent all of his salary on his mother's operation. He knew he may be killed if he came up, lost the fight, and couldn't pay. But he realized he couldn't pass up the opportunity. "I needed it, needed it, needed it," Gunn declares. "I was nervous by myself, but my mother was dying." "I needed the money.

The next night, Gunn drove his father's white Dodge van to the gym, leaving his pit bull, Duran, in the front seat, and entered to find a hundred people, largely bikers, waiting for the show. His opponent, 6'2", 200 pounds or more, and severely tattooed, stood in the ring wearing jeans and boots. Gunn removed his shirt and wore only acid-wash denim and black Reeboks. The bikers weren't impressed. "The guy started laughing at me, calling me a little kid," Gunn says. "His teammates yelled, 'Don't kill this punk!'"

The management sounded the bell, and the fight started. It did not last long. The biker rushed Gunn, who twisted and clipped him many times in the middle. The man became enraged and began shooting randomly as the young gypsy picked him apart. "He's on his knees, blood pouring out of him, and the manager comes and raises my hand," Gunn tells me. "Do you know what I was thinking about?" I had my mother's Doulton dolls and Dresden plates in the van, which were her pride and joy as an elderly gypsy woman. Probably worth about ten grand, and I was intending to sell them to a pawn shop to make money."

Gunn pauses.

"I wasn't worried about the fight," he jokes. "I was worried about someone stealing those dolls."

The end came quickly.

Jackie had a liver transplant and appeared to be doing well. Then, one night, Gunn and his father were summoned to the hospital from their nearby motel. According to Gunn, a hospital trainee attempting to perform a liver biopsy ruptured Jackie's stitches on the internal organ, causing her heart to fail due to shock and discomfort. "She had a massive heart attack while squealing in pain with a tube down her throat," he tells me. "My mom never had any easy going."

Gunn and his father wanted to return Jackie to Canada while still respecting her family's desires. So, in the winter of 1993, they interred her on her family's plot in Baltimore. Jackie's Irish Traveler kin attended both a Catholic and a Protestant service. The mood was tight. "It was a big, big funeral," Gunn adds. "Must have been a thousand gypsies there." With his last $300, Gunn bought a boxing belt and had it engraved "Champion of the Universe, My Old Mom: The Toughest Fighter I Ever Knew." He placed it atop the casket as the bagpipes played "Amazing Grace." Some of the Linsday clan objected to the belt, calling it disrespectful, nearly starting a brawl right there at the funeral. "Dad said, 'You cocksuckers, walk now or you're going to be in there with her,'" Gunn fondly remembers. "The old man flipped out. "This was his little wife, the love of his life."

After the service, Gunn borrowed money from one of his uncles, loaded his sad father and the dog into his pickup truck, and traveled south. Gunn's life had been wrecked during the last two years, so he was leaving with his remaining family for a remote Traveler outpost in Florida, a place of palm trees and beach and bright, thoughtless sun—a place where he could start over. "King wanted me to fight a guy and told me, 'It's your breakthrough fight; it'll put you on top of the world,'" he said. "But I just got a dirty, rotten, disgusted feeling with the whole game when I buried Mom."

Gunn kept all he owned in his pickup truck. He had his clothes, his boxing gear, and a small piece of paper from the gym manager in Pittsburgh that included the phone number of a man who could get him additional underground fights—bigger fights—if he wanted.

Gunn didn't step inside a boxing ring for another eleven years.

CHAPTER 9
TRADING GLOVES FOR LOVE

*B*obby Gunn assured his wife he was done fighting.

Gunn moved to Fort Lauderdale, Florida, in the winter of 1993, devastated by his mother's death and the abrupt collapse of his boxing career, and fell in love. He had met Rose Keith, a gorgeous blond Scottish Traveler, while boxing in Las Vegas, and she had never left his mind since. Rose was glamorous and gregarious, and she hailed from an affluent real estate family. Hugh, her father, owned twenty mobile-home parks and was so successful that the family had settled down. "All the Traveler kids were out visiting in Vegas," Gunn remembers when he first met Rose. "I only remember she was stunning. But she was among the privileged. She did not go to T.J. Maxx. She headed to Neiman Marcus. I didn't think I'd have a chance." Rose had grown up with everything Gunn lacked—money, security, a fixed residence, unconditional affection, even box seats to Dolphins games—and would appear an improbable fit. Hugh, a 6'5" hard-nosed businessman, had formerly been a knucklehead, and Gunn's reputation as a boxer lent credibility.

"In the Traveler community, sometimes that means more than money," Ruml adds.

For Gunn, Rose was a lifeline. In Florida, without boxing or Jackie to keep them together, he and his father had grown apart, with despair looming over their modest flat on the outskirts of town. Gunn and Robert would occasionally go to the local gym to shadow box or work the pads, hoping to reestablish some semblance of normalcy. But not even training—the one communion they had always shared—could shake them out of their rut. "Dad was bad," Gunn remembers. "And I just broke away from boxing."

Gunn abandoned the fighting scene to pursue a new goal: love. "I never even had a girlfriend before Rose," he jokes. "To me, she was a princess." Gunn's courtship of Rose, like so many parts of Traveler society, was straight out of the Middle Ages—he could have come with a lute beneath her balcony. Travelers do not date, and certainly do not engage in premarital sex. Instead, teenagers must interact in groups during weekends. So, one night at a Benihana, after only two months of brief discussions in the throng, Gunn approached Rose and asked for her hand. "That Elvis song 'Only Fools Rush In' was playing," Gunn recalls. "And I just blurted, 'I think you're gorgeous and want to marry you.'" "I'll be good to you," she murmured, shook my hand, and kissed me.

To finalize the engagement, Gunn went to meet Rose's parents and invited them to breakfast at Denny's. "Her folks pull up in a big Mercedes 500, wearing Rolex watches," Gunn tells me. "I get out of my work truck in an old leather jacket and say, 'I'm Bobby Gunn.' And her dad just says, 'I know who you are.'" In the tight-knit Traveler world, Gunn knew that Rose's parents would have heard about his years as a pro boxer and his courtship, and that they were weighing his family background and intentions. Nervous yet determined, he told his story over eggs and pancakes. "They look at me and think, 'This is a fighter, and he has nothing. Is he going to be a deadbeat? Is he going to torment my girlfriend?"Gunn recalls. "So I said, 'I'll be honest with you. I love your girl, and I vow to God I will never touch her. My mother just died. I do not have much. But I'll give it a shot in life." Gunn sat back, silently staring at Rose's parents across the Formica tabletop. After a few moments, her father, Hugh, said. "He just says, 'Gamest words I've ever heard any young man say,'" Gunn recollects. "And he shook my hand." Gunn smiles. "They respected me."

Finally, after six weeks of intense hand-holding supervised by family members, Gunn, then twenty-one, was set to marry Rose, nineteen.

His courage had paid off. There was still one more obstacle to cross. Rose reached Gunn in the final days before the ceremony, insisting on one more condition: he gave up the gloves. "She never wanted to see me fight," Gunn explains. "It bothered her." Gunn's reputation as a fighter had earned him the respect of her family, but not her. So, already exhausted from boxing and completely in love, he agreed to leave the combat game. "I thought she was too good for me," he admits. "I was tickled to death." I simply responded, 'Let's give it a go.'"

Gunn felt peaceful for the first time in his life. "I never had any brothers or sisters," he maintains. "Compassion, for me, came entirely from my mother. So having someone like Rose opened up a new portion of my heart that I was wanting to discover. I could trust her. She was a godsend.

After a brief honeymoon at Disney World, he and Rose moved into an apartment at Sawgrass Mills Mall and settled into a suburban lifestyle surrounded by Florida's sunlight, ocean spray, and flowers. Following Traveler custom, he went to work at his father's trade, pouring asphalt along vine-draped, alligator-infested roads, while Rose cared for the house and managed their finances. When he returned home at night, he would frequently surprise her with a new dress purchased at a nearby boutique. On weekends, he took Rose to Orlando or went hunting with his father-in-law in the Everglades, where he once shot a massive tusked boar only to have an even larger alligator come along and eat his trophy. In the subtropics, away from the cold and chaos of his upbringing, Gunn began to move on from his mother's death and the loss of his work, finding surprising fulfillment in a stable home. "It changed his life," explains Ed Simpson, a Traveler and family friend. "He finally found love and a normal life."

Gunn's marriage also emancipated him from his father. A month after the ceremony, Robert surprised him with the news that he was coming home to Niagara Falls. "After my wife died, I had to be alone for a while," Robert explains. "I couldn't train Bobby, and everything had gone wrong."

Gunn's departure was surprising. "When I got married, Dad told me 'Good man' and shook my hand," according to him. "When I returned to see him, he said, 'You're a man now.'" You made your bed, and you must sleep in it. He even took my dog, Duran."

Gunn had conflicting feelings about his father leaving. Robert was his sole remaining near relative. In the end, exhausted from years of prizefighting and his mother's illness—and possibly from his father's drinking and sinking spells—Gunn felt it was time to strike out on his own. "Me and Rose just made a go of it," adds the man. "Fridays are for movies, Saturdays are for work, and Sundays are for church. "Life was fun."

Yet something continued to chew at him. He hailed from a family of fighters, had brawled his entire life, and couldn't stop missing the ring. He also felt obligated to produce more money, to provide Rose with the life she had given up—even if it meant breaching their wedding-night commitment. "My wife kept the fire under my ass," he tells me. "I couldn't just be a normal guy, because she was used to having high things."

So, when a Traveler asked Gunn if he wanted to make money in an underground bare-knuckle fight, he didn't hesitate—even when told he'd have to fight two guys in a row. "I said, 'We'll have a little fun,'" he explains.

The following night, after claiming Rose was going to the gym, Gunn traveled to a dilapidated warehouse in South Beach, Miami, to face the two local boxers. South Beach in the early 1990s was a wasteland, a saltwater melting pot of drifters and immigrant Cubans eking out a livelihood amid squalid hotels, boarded-up warehouses, and crumbling Art Deco structures, devoid of its current revived sheen. In the darkened warehouse, with the smell of sea and perspiration in the air, Gunn battled the guys in consecutive fights in a small ring in front of a large crowd of Cubans, other Latinos, and motorcyclists. "We fought right off the ocean," Gunn explains. "Broken windows and glass was everywhere." His years of sparring with the world's top boxing champions were immediately apparent. "They were dumplings," he says about his opponents. "Out cold. "Bang-bang." He left with $1,500 cash.

Gunn didn't understand it at the time, but he had just entered what would become his true calling, a world he had only glimpsed a few months before at a biker fight in Pittsburgh as his mother lay dying— a world he would now join full-time: the underground. "That's the first time I really saw the circuit," he boasts, "but it was here long before I was born."

The underground, a patchwork of regional promoters and combatants as diverse as the states themselves, is a dark reflection of America. Whether it's with gangbangers in Los Angeles, ranchers in Texas, Native Americans in Arizona, or good ol' boys in Mississippi, fights can vary greatly in feel, custom, and audience. However, one fact stays constant. The more populous East Coast has the most fights— and its epicenter is New York, where the best boxers compete for more money than anywhere else. "All the best fighters go to New York," Gunn explains. "Manhattan, Queens, Brooklyn, the Bronx— the underground circuit brings them all there."

Gunn had strayed into Gotham's raw, sweltering shadow realm, the polar opposite of the East Coast's bare-knuckle experience. In the underworld, Florida serves as a sort of proving ground, a significant feeder system where fighters come up brawling in backyard bouts all year, building a reputation that will take them across the country.

"South Florida is kinda like the old days in New York," says Guy

Pagan, 58, a boxing promoter and former army ranger who attends underground fights in Miami. "You have a lot of immigrants. But instead of Irish, there are Mexicans, Puerto Ricans, and Dominicans. Every now and then, a guy will fly in from somewhere and want to test the waters. Like a nasty guy who just ran over everyone in Mississippi. Big white dude gets out of the car, and you're like, "Holy shiiittt, look at this dude!"And he wants to scrap. And some of these individuals are white supremacists, thugs, and they say it in black and white: 'Let's go down there and fuck with these niggers.'"

In Florida's underground underworld, no one supervises more bare-knuckle bouts than Dhafir Harris, a former correctional officer known as Dada 5000. Harris, 39, has long staged bare-knuckle fights in his grandmother's garden in south Miami, turning local gang bosses into hired brawlers. "People are robbed and killed here every day," Harris claims. "These guys are amateur boxers, football players, brawlers, and wannabes, all just fighting for a way out." Florida's most renowned bare-knuckle export is Kevin Ferguson, often known as Kimbo Slice. Slice, a 6'2" 230-pound Bahamian fighter raised in South Miami, briefly played linebacker on the Miami Dolphins practice squad before becoming homeless, living in his car, and eventually achieving renown on YouTube for his bare-knuckle clashes. These gory brawls include a thirteen-minute bout with a Boston cop that landed him a contract with the Ultimate Fighting Championship (UFC). Slice passed away from heart failure in 2016, at the age of 42. However, in his dying months, the aged street champion had planned to return to his roots in a bare-knuckle bout against Gunn on his own soil. "All fighters love Florida," Harris says. "But we didn't invent this—it's been around since the gladiator days."

Gunn started creating his own reputation in Florida in 1994, shortly after his double knockdown in Miami. By day, he would pour asphalt and paint structures. By night, he would look for local bouts, usually taking on one every several months. South Florida, a melting pot of Cubans, Blacks, Puerto Ricans, and whites, was rife with international drug money, and traffickers and dealers supported dogfights, cockfights, and, where possible, bare-knuckles. Gunn battled in backyards, abandoned swimming pools, and warehouses. He battled in restaurants, nightclubs, and private residences. He fought both alone and on other fighters' cards, in midday and night contests. Throughout, he kept his rising name in the underworld hidden from Rose, returning home with gifts and outfits while telling her he was sparring in gyms to stay fit. "I'd come back with a small black eye, and she'd ask, 'What happened?'" he says. "'Tough workout.'"

Of all Gunn's early underground battles, none compare to one of his first huge money matches, a fight against a motorcyclist in a parking lot behind a bar off I-75 in west Fort Lauderdale—a stretch of highway known as Alligator Alley. The fight occurred in the afternoon. The lot was packed with perhaps 75 individuals, and the air was thick with the odor of sweat and heated beer. "I'd been painting roofs and was wearing my painter's shorts," according to Gunn. "The back of the place was like a wrecker's yard of cars and trucks." As usual, Gunn arrived unaware of his opponent's identity. All he knew was the amount of the prize money: $10,000. After being notified by his opponent's supporters, he paid his original security deposit of $2,000, or 20% "kick-in" money, to a third party and now strolled in with the balance in a bag, flanked by two Travelers. When he entered the lot, he noticed his opponent—a muscle-bound 6 '2", 225-pound biker accompanied by twenty-five of his mates, a wandering militia of tattoos and leather jackets.

"We were like, 'Oh shit, where is the exit?'" says Ed Simpson, a Traveler who was with Gun that day. "It must have been a hundred degrees, with sweat flowing off you. And I was terrified: 'Man, if Bobby kills this man, will we make it out alive? Or will these guys kill us?'There was a lot of money on the line. But it didn't disturb Bobby. He said, 'All right, bring it on.'"

The motorcyclist came out swinging, and the audience cheered. "They thought they had it in the bag," Simpson adds. "We're talking about a big dude, brother—a lot bigger than Bobby." To the crowd's surprise, Gunn avoided the biker's shots, each of which had the potential to knock him out, while waiting, watching, and getting to know his opponent. The two men traded a few more hits, Gunn's fists appearing to have no impact, before the shot that sent the audience into a frenzy. The biker punched Gunn three times in a succession, nearly knocking him over. "They were really good shots," Simpson explains. "Kinda shook Bobby a little bit."

Gunn embraced the biker, and the two guys held on to one other for fifteen seconds to gather their breath before separating. Looking for the kill, the biker moved in for another potential knockout punch—and made his deadly mistake. Gunn sidestepped his hook and hit him with a rapid combination: a left to the body, which stunned his opponent and caused him to drop his arms, followed by a right to the temple. The biker fell. "It went from yelling and cheering to dead silence," Simpson explains. "Weirdest thing you've ever seen in your life." Without hesitation, Gunn grabbed the money and walked away. "Stick around too long," he jokes, "and they'll get buyer's remorse."

For a few years after his triumph in Alligator Alley, Gunn continued to fight around Florida, with no one noticing his background. "At first, I could throw my hat in the mix and get in fights anywhere," he recounts. "They didn't know who I was, so I could slip in like a pool shark and take you to school." He doesn't answer. "It was good for me. Young guy, married, came home with $10,000 in my pocket. It made my marriage much nicer. And Rose thought I was out working."

CHAPTER 10
TO THE TOP, FALLING HARD

By 2005, Gunn was commanding a $10,000 challenge fee in the underground—often the bare minimum for just showing up. Capitalizing on his growing popularity, he traveled increasingly far for big-money fights, battling in warehouses in downtown Los Angeles, backyard contests in Phoenix, and empty lots in Tennessee, Ohio, and Michigan. He occasionally took on bouts since he was passing through the area on business. Occasionally, he drove or flew particularly for fights. "The guys who put on these fights all know who Bobby is," states Paul Tyler. "Could be a gym owner, a connected guy, a rich guy, a regular guy trying to put these on—but a lot of them can't afford Bobby."

While working near the Mexican border, Gunn once brawled in the late afternoon light among the cacti and sagebrush on a property outside Corpus Christi, Texas. Gunn was the main attraction at a rancher-staged event that drew a huge gathering of local whites and Hispanics. "The promoter was this cowboy I'd met at a bare-knuckle fight in Boston," says Tyler, who flew out for the event with his own boxers. "They were planning a big fight, and Bobby was out there working with the gypsies." The cowboy stated that he usually does not bring people out; they do their own thing out there, but, you know, everyone knows Bobby." Gunn fought off against his opponent in front of a crowd of Travelers who were passing through the lower Rio Grande Valley for work. "I fought a cowboy guy, a nice kid," Gunn explains. "Dropped him in approximately 30 seconds. Just didn't have much in him."

When big-money fights got rough and tumble, Gunn battled harder. "Grab the tip of the ear and it rips right off," according to him. "Take your thumb and poke it in someone's eye—done it many times."

Once, in a parking lot bout in Camden, New Jersey, while suffocating in a headlock, Gunn reached down, removed his opponent's balls, and then whirled around to bite his ear and end him with punches." In a warehouse battle in Brooklyn, he once launched a corkscrew punch so strong that it knocked a man's eyeball out of its socket, the organ "swelling out like an egg" before hanging by a vein. Years later, Gunn ran across this man again, now sporting an eye patch, when he filled Gunn's truck with gas at a wayside station near Hackensack, New Jersey. "I thought he was going to try to murder me," Gunn admits. "But he was excited: 'Hi, Bobby!'""

But, of all his rough-and-tumble fights, Gunn's most high-stakes encounter was against a former NFL star in a match arranged by various Latino gangs in a Bronx warehouse in 2007. Gunn came in the early evening, dressed in his typical muscle shirt and acid-wash pants, to discover perhaps a hundred people drinking and gambling. The event was a social gathering with tequila and bare-knuckle fights. Gunn was the headliner. "These guys were all blinged out," admits underground promoter Paul Tyler, who was with Gun that day. "A few parts were flashed. There was a cashout. Guys are smoking cannabis. It looked like some kind of Colombian cocaine."

Gunn removed his shirt and strode into the midst of the gathering. His opponent was a 6'1" 220-pound Black male wearing shorts and a tank top. According to Tyler, the brawler was a former linebacker who played two years of college, briefly competed in the NFL, and then attempted to become a professional boxer. Perhaps he viewed bare knuckles as a new opportunity. "I believe he'd had one pro boxing fight at that point," Tyler tells me. "He was there to win."

Gunn started out swinging but struggled to reach the linebacker, who towered above him and had a longer reach. In response, the linebacker launched large, ponderous punches, hoping to finish the battle with a knockout. Gunn effortlessly evaded them, and the crowd became animated—this was going to be an exciting fight. For five minutes, the two men moved around the lot, jabbing and ducking, occasionally landing bullets. The linebacker was causing damage to Gunn, connecting on strong shots. However, Gunn was landing several of his own. Slowly, the linebacker began to tire, and the momentum changed. Finally, Gunn dropped him. "And that's when he bit him," Tyler recalls.

After being counted out, the linebacker stood and approached Gunn, arms outstretched as if for an embrace. Then the huge football player did something no one expected. He craned his neck and bit into Gunn's meaty neck. "He went, 'Harhn,'" Gunn says, making a gnawing sound. "I went, 'Oh, you fucking cunt.'" Gunn grabbed the linebacker, hauled him up, and bit a quarter-sized hole in his cheek. Gunn, still clutching him, used his teeth to rip the top of his ear completely off.

"I mean, like a fucking animal," Tyler says. "It started gushing and there was a mess on the ground, and everyone just said, 'Woah!'" Gunn spat out the man's ear, pounded him with four blows, and threw him to the ground. The linebacker's supporters cried foul, but the organizers intervened to resolve the situation, pointing out that their man had bitten first. Gunn came away with a hole in his neck and $20,000, his largest purse to date.

Gunn, who had made a fortune from his underground battles, could now fund his pro boxing comeback. Competing as a cruiserweight, weighing in at a lean, shredded 190 pounds, he spent hours at Ike's gym sparring, lifting, and hobbling on the treadmill to keep his fighting form. "Even though my leg was bad, I was in good shape," Gunn claims. "I knew I could pull something off."

Following his debut victory in Greensboro, North Carolina, Gunn immediately took on another confidence-building contest in an undercard bout against Earl Kirkendall, a thirty-eight-year-old amateur champion with only one pro fight (a loss) under his belt.

Gunn returned to the ring for the second time in eleven years in February 2005, at Nashville's 9,200-seat municipal auditorium. "I'll never forget it," said Joe Mack, his promoter at the time. "Bobby struck this guy with a left hook to the body that sounded like a drum hit. The entire crowd exclaimed, 'Oh! 'And the guy went down—that started our journey."

Continuing his win streak against low-tier opponents in Mack's backyard—the South—Gunn defeated guys like Jimmy Garrett, a forty-five-year-old journeyman with a 3-28 record, in Memphis, and Jeff Holcomb, an Iraq War vet and police officer with a 10-3 record from Fort Oglethorpe, Georgia, before taking on his first major fight, against Shelby Gross for the International Boxing Association cruiserweight title belt, in Nashville in March 2006. While not one of boxing's primary titles, the IBA belt was a decent stepping-stone triumph for champions like Oscar De La Hoya, Roy Jones Jr., and James Toney on their road to the top. For Gunn, it signified everything, and now, with a 15-2 career record, he felt ready to face a true opponent. "I was feeling good," Gunn explains. "Knocked Jeff out in the fifth round, broke his spleen, and spilled blood on the canvas. What a hammering I dealt him. And then the corruption began anew."

Shelby Gross, a roughhouse boxer from South Carolina with a 16-3 record, came to the battle carrying baggage. In 2000, he wore a wire to a meeting with Las Vegas promoter Robert Mitchell, taped Mitchell's attempt to bribe him with $8,000 to lose a match, and then turned over the evidence to the FBI. The taped meeting resulted in a string of fighter arrests, as well as the first conviction of a boxer for a fight-fixing scheme in Nevada.

That ordeal, however, would soon be eclipsed by Gross's fight against Gunn—"one of the wildest affairs ever seen in a professional ring," according to the IBA. In front of a screaming crowd at Music City's nine-thousand-seat Municipal Auditorium, Gunn and Gross fought with abandon, exchanging haymakers and knockout shots while careening across the ring. In the opening round, Gunn knocked Gross down twice. Then, in the second, the South Carolina boxer returned the favor, felling Gunn, pouncing on him, and beating him with shots—a wholly illegal move—until the referee snatched Gross up and body-slammed him to the ground. Unable to recover from the illegal beating, Gunn was eventually knocked flat on his back as the bell rang. The referee proclaimed Gross the winner via technical knockout, and his entourage swarmed the ring in celebration. However, the victory would not last long. Gross failed a drug test for an illegal substance the following month, resulting in a no-contest ruling by the Tennessee Athletic Commission—a decision backed by an angry IBA and national Association of Boxing Commissions over the bout's sloppy refereeing. "The integrity of this event [was] somewhere between 'ear biting' and 'post fight mugging,'" the IBA stated.

Gunn was outraged, ashamed, and heartbroken after the bout, which turned his one shot at a world title into a weird show. "I was shell shocked," he says. Six months later, Joe Mack scheduled him to fight again for the same IBA world title, this time against Shannon "the Sandman" Landberg, a respected veteran with a 58-11 record, in the Lac Courte Oreilles Reservation in northern Wisconsin. Landberg, 41, was even more washed up than Gunn. However, the clean-shaven, muscle-bound former army boxer had never won a world title and was determined to defeat Gunn. "Landberg was a very cagey guy, a veteran," Gunn says. "And I had just broken my thumb."

Gunn had been sparring a few days before the bout when he caught his right thumb in his opponent's headgear, shattering it at the tip. "The skin was just holding it together," Gunn explains. "It went black." Knowing he couldn't pass the state medical inspection for the fight with a fractured, blackened thumb, Gunn covered up his injuries with cosmetics from his wife's purse. When the half-distracted doctor yanked on it during his examination, Gunn bit his lip to prevent from weeping. "I thought I was going to bite my fucking tongue in two," he tells me. "Oh, the pain." Gunn was used to battling with a broken wing. "I went into a lot of fights with broken hands," he recalls. "To keep the doctor's mind off any thought of injury, I'd grab his hand and shake it right—that was always the most nerve-racking part."

Cleared for the battle, Gunn entered the arena in tartan trunks and trailed a lone bagpiper he'd hired for the occasion. He was determined to win the belt. For the first few rounds, cradling his right hand, he fought largely with his left, pulling Sandberg apart. Then, when his adrenaline surged, Gunn claims he stopped experiencing pain. "It sounds weird, but sometimes that happens," he informs me. "The right hand starts numbing and the swelling acts like a case—I started plugging away with it." Now blending his bare-knuckle street tactics with boxing skills, Gunn landed jab after jab while also throwing in a few shots below the belt and even headbutting Landberg at one point, which resulted in the penalty. In reaction, Landberg fired power bullets from close range, causing cuts above Gunn's eyes. Both men were sweating and bleeding on the canvas as the Midwestern crowd applauded. In the end, Gunn won. "By the fifth round, I felt the life leaving him, and by the sixth I knew it was a matter of time," according to Gunn. "I broke him down." Landberg, who was struggling with a cracked tooth and a fractured right eye socket, threw in the towel just 36 seconds into round seven. Gunn was awarded the new IBA cruiserweight world champion. "I reached down and put my boy on my shoulders," Gunn tells me. "Once a champ, always a champ."

That night, Gunn shared a double room with his father-in-law, Hugh Keith, and Bobby Jr. (Gunn's father, Robert, had not arrived.) Sleeping in the same bed as his son, Gunn placed the huge belt between them, watching as the youngster fell asleep with the trophy in his hands. "I stayed up until two in the morning, just looking at my wee boy and reminiscing on the fight," Gunn shares. "Becoming a world champion for my son was priceless—there's no money that could beat that night."

The victory propelled Gunn into the top fifteen national rankings, capping an extraordinary run by the aging unknown. Just two years after restarting his career, Gunn was given a chance at true stardom in an HBO broadcast battle against Enzo Maccarinelli, the 6'4", 200-pound Welsh cruiserweight champion, in a World Boxing Organization title bout at Cardiff, Wales' 74,000-seat Principality Stadium. Maccarinelli's opponent withdrew at the last minute, making way for Gunn, who, although being written off by the UK press, regarded this as his long-awaited moment for triumph. "This is my shot," he remarked in an interview. "I've got a couple more years to make the best of it and I feel like a million dollars." 7

If Gunn's IBA belt was seen as a stepping stone, the WBO title was the ultimate prize—one of only four world championships recognized by the International Boxing Hall of Fame. Gunn had been flown in by powerful UK promoter Frank Warren for the bout against Maccarinelli, a twenty-six-year-old hometown favorite and emerging European star raised just down the road in Swansea, on the undercard of Joe Calzaghe, another local champion. Trying to gain popularity with US fans, Maccarinelli, the son of an Italian immigrant boxer trying to increase his record after a pair of huge matches fell through, faced Gunn as the strong favorite. "I have had a few disappointments in the past year," Maccarinelli stated at the time. "But I'm focusing on my frustration and getting in shape for my life. ..Soon enough, I will be the main man, and Bobby Gunn will find out.

When Gunn arrived in Cardiff in April 2007, he realized something was wrong right away. Travelers have long been mocked in Wales and around the UK—and on the day of the fight, he arrived at the stadium to discover an especially hostile crowd. "People yelling, calling me pikey," Gunn adds, referring to the ethnic epithet for Travelers. "It was horrible." He was then handed a memo by management. Gunn would have to replace his trunks because they were too close in color to Macarinelli's. One more thing: he would have to prepare for the battle in a public bathroom. In boxing, underdog opponents are frequently treated as second-class citizens by promoters attempting to give their starfighters an advantage, employing a variety of strategies to degrade their opponents. However, Gunn and his supporters argue that the battle in Wales was over the top.

"These promoters pull all sorts of tricks," says Mike Hopper, Gunn's cut man in the fight. "When we arrived, all jet-lagged, they crammed five grown guys into a small car and drove us around the hills for about three hours before delivering us to the motel—and, needless to say, the amenities were terrible. Sometimes they put something in your food to give you the runs. Hell, I had one fighter have three hookers come to his door the night before his bout to throw him off—the A guy gets the hotel, and the B guy gets the shithouse."

Gritting his teeth, Gunn, then 33, strolled into the stadium's bowels, located a bench in a concrete public lavatory, and slipped on his backup trunks and gloves as a steady stream of drunken people passed by to use the urinals. "Here comes a drunk to take a piss as I'm getting my hands wrapped," Gunn tells me. "'Good luck, mate!'"

When asked about the fight, Gunn will confess that he was outboxed. However, he claims that was the strategy. "The whole plan was to let Enzo punch himself out," he claims. According to Gunn and his staff, he planned to lose the first few rounds in the hopes of exhausting Maccarinelli, leaving him vulnerable to a knockout punch. Gunn believes that the battle was called off too soon.

However, seeing the battle on YouTube for two minutes and thirty-five seconds makes it impossible to believe Gunn had any chance. Finally, a fighter who loses a match will undoubtedly claim that he was robbed. He must assign blame; modesty may practically kill a man in the ring. However, in Gunn's case, the universal judgment was clear: the veteran journeyman fighter had simply gotten in over his head. "The eccentric American pug Bobby Gunn," concluded British boxing journalist David Payne. "A fighter plucked from obscurity." ..and then plunged back into the tank-town circuit following his one-round slaughter at the hands of the towering Welshman."

In the end, Gunn exited the battle injured, bruised, and embarrassed—he had failed miserably in his one big chance on the international stage. "I mean, we were on HBO, man," Mack explains. "That was humiliating. It was challenging for him."

There would be one advantage, however. Morose in the motel room, cooling his wounds and waiting for the cab trip to the airport, Gunn was approached by his father, who had been drinking all day. "Told ya," Robert remarked, sitting next to him with a cigarette dangling out of his mouth. "The fix is in. "You got fucked, boy."

Gunn remained still, not saying anything, replaying the battle in his mind, wondering what he could have done differently. "I was mad at myself," he admits. He didn't want to hear his father exult. Surprisingly, his father opened out. "He said he was proud of me and kissed me," Gunn recalls. "He was more of a father at that point than before. 'Hold your head up and go out of here,' he commanded me. 'You're a fighting Traveler man.'"

Gunn would never fight another international match.

CHAPTER 11
A FIGHT FOR GLORY

*I*n June 2011, David Feldman had a life-changing notion. Gunn may not have been a world boxing champion, but he did have something no one else did: the best underground record. "Love it or hate it, bare knuckle always gets people excited," according to Feldman. "I knew this could be my way out."

Feldman had spent his whole life hustling, pushing every type of fight sport possible in every low-tier casino across the country, and he had almost nothing to show for it. But this was different. This was an opportunity to create his own sport, to legitimize bare-knuckle fighting, and to follow in the footsteps of his hero, Dana White, the visionary who helped transform the UFC from an outlaw competition into a $12 billion global phenomenon. This was a chance to build an empire. He already had a built-in star.

But first he needed to persuade Gunn to do it.

"I was nervous," Gunn remembers, when he first heard of bare-knuckle fighting in public. "I didn't think this was something we needed to bring attention to."

Feldman knew otherwise. "I love Bobby, but he doesn't understand business," he replies. "He's always thinking about how to get $5,000 tonight. But I'm working on how to make $5 million next year."

He grins.

"I knew this could be my last hustle."

The crazy thing is, Feldman has a chance.

Pro boxing, which began in smoky gambling dens in the nineteenth century and was never properly structured at the national level, is still the only major sport in the United States that lacks a central regulatory authority. It has no equivalent to the modern NFL, NBA, or MLB. Instead, the multibillion-dollar sport, like all other fight disciplines, is administered by a slew of sanctioning bodies that have formed over time, each issuing its own championship belts and overseen by independent state athletic commissions. These state commissions can choose to connect with the national Association of Boxing Commissions, the closest counterpart to a central regulatory body, but this is a voluntary decision, implying that the fight world is largely governed at the state level.

In fact, only in recent decades has there been any kind of national control, with the Professional Boxing Safety Act of 1996 and the Muhammad Ali Boxing Reform Act of 2000 providing some measure of safety for fighters' health—but no safeguards for their fair pay. According to Feldman, it all boils down to one fundamental truth: "This is the biggest scumbag business in the world." "Every day it's a fight."

Even Greg Sirb, the stern Pennsylvania state sports commissioner, concurs: "It's a billion-dollar industry run like a five-and-dime store."

Fighting's lack of oversight has had an advantage, though. It has produced one of the most promising chances in professional sports: a lawless landscape with no central regulatory body, allowing new leagues to emerge. It paved the way for the UFC, the most unlikely success story in sports history. And Feldman believes that the fight world's chaotic nature will catapult bare knuckles to respectability and glory.

After all, far more unlikely combat sports have existed before. In the fighting arena, new tournaments emerge every few years, usually in poorer countries with less to lose. The UFC, for example, hosted some of its early events in Oklahoma, Wyoming, and Alabama. In

2015, South Carolina legalized arena fighting, a sport that originated as a Russian game show in which two-man MMA teams sprint, jump, and fight each other on a padded obstacle course, resembling a group brawl at a gymnastics center. Imported by former MMA fighter Casey Oxendine, the sport was pitched around to various state commissions before South Carolina finally agreed. (In contrast, Andy Foster of the California State Athletic Commission stated, "We're saying no, and there's a period behind the no.")1

The trick to starting a new fight sport isn't winning federal politicians' approval. The trick is to find a state athletic commission that is willing to take a chance on being the first taxpayer-funded entity to approve your creation and will stick with you through bad press, irate governors, political pressure from the national commission, and the threat of lawsuits if someone is injured at your premier event. Even then, there is no certainty. After two sanctioned contests in Myrtle Beach, arena combat failed to garner national traction and retreated back to Siberia. "It's hard," adds UFC founder Art Davie. "Everybody says you're crazy."

But Feldman had a plan. Even though it was bloody, bare knuckle fighting proved to be safer than boxing or mixed martial arts. Despite its reputation for attracting unruly barroom brawlers, it frequently included professional fighters, many of whom were retired from other fight sports but could still handle the rapid gloveless rounds. And, perhaps most crucially, bare knuckle had an unlawful reputation, an illegal blood-soaked mystique linked to US history—and it might just break through to cynical Millennials looking for the next extreme sport. "If Dave Feldman stays in it for the long haul, he could make a billion bucks," according to Davie. "Now that audiences are habituated to more violence, he needs to increase the cruelty. He wants to get the eighteen-year-olds to look up from their phones and say, 'Hey, that's cool.' In the end, promoting is truly about developing a brand—he needs to create a hero."

Feldman found his hero in June 2011, but getting him to fight proved difficult. Gunn had been supporting his family with asphalt labor and the underground for the two years since his heartbreaking loss to Tomasz Adamek, and he was concerned that the Arizona match would draw unwanted attention, interrupting his underground income. But more importantly, Gunn had simply lost his motivation. His boxing return had been a remarkable effort—the middle-aged journeyman progressing from high school gyms to state fairgrounds to world-class arenas—but it was now done. Gunn would never become a world champion boxer. So he did what he had done over twenty years before: hung up his gloves and returned full-time to the only place he had ever known: the subterranean.

"Because of the way that Adamek fight ended, he just wanted to get back into bare knuckle," says Joe "Mack" McEwen, Gunn's previous promoter. "He decided to stop cutting weight and just fight at his natural weight, a heavyweight." Now muscled and calm, out of the harsh limelight and making top money on the bare-knuckle circuit, Gunn could easily have turned down Arizona. But there was one more reason to say yes: the prospect of becoming a top-tier world champion in at least one combat sport.

"I would be recognized as the bare-knuckle world heavyweight champion," Gunn shares. "Bare knuckle was in my family blood, and Dave saw an opportunity."

Since their first meeting, Gunn and Feldman had been close, albeit argumentative, friends. Feldman had sponsored numerous of Gunn's pro boxing contests, including manning his corner for the Adamek fight, while the Traveler champion had continued to educate his "country-person" friend on the underground, taking Feldman to bare-knuckle fights across the Northeast.

The sardonic, cynical promoter and his Christ-loving boxer made for a funny pairing. Feldman would go underground for weeks, refusing

95

to return calls, only to resurface full of sarcasm and jibes, taunting Gunn and occasionally going too far. While going through a divorce, Feldman began cursing Gunn on the lawn of his Philadelphia home, eventually firing a jab at the bare-knuckle champion, who returned with a strong body hit, crumpling the promoter to the ground. Another occasion, while the two men were sharing a hotel room in Scotland for a meeting with promoters, Feldman kept rubbing Gunn until 4:00 a.m. For no apparent reason, the warrior eventually lost it and split his friend's nose. "That's Dave; it's his personality," Gunn replies, shrugging. "I can't figure him out."

But Gunn knows one thing: Feldman is present when it counts. The two men come from similar backgrounds, have troubled connections with their fathers, and frequently confide in one another, even crying and opening up before returning to their normal bickering. "My old man was crazy and rough and he was hard and cold," according to Gunn. "I've always known Dave was a top man." After the Adamek match, Feldman did not pay Gunn his part of $30,000 for nearly a week, dismissing him. But, just as Gunn was ready to apprehend him, Feldman showed up with the entire sum, refusing to accept even his own 10% part of the deal. "He just wanted to see if I'd flip out," Gunn adds. "Yes, Dave has an attitude, and I've had to rough him up a little bit. But I've always known he's with me all the way."

For his part, Feldman will tell you that Gunn can be an incessant bother, nagging him daily about getting pro boxing matches and then turning up with a swarm of Travelers, many of whom try to sneak in for free. "Scumbags," Feldman retorts. However, when pressed, he will shrug and say, "Yeah, Bobby's like a brother to me. He'll tell me to go fuck myself, I'll tell him to go fuck himself, and we'll be friends. It's one of those things." There's only one catch, one unbreakable line that will always separate them. "Bobby does not understand business at all," Feldman claims. "He becomes impatient. I have to remind him of the UFC, how it took years to get started properly, and how if we just make 10 percent of that, we'll be a home run, so we need to start acting like that. But he's never going to get it, and that's good. But he needs to let me do my job."

Even before approaching Gunn in 2011, Feldman needed to secure a venue, and he knew just one place that was willing to support him: the Yavapai Nation. In 2008, the tribe was thrilled by Gunn's ability to attract hordes of Travelers for his boxing battle, and they quickly inquired about his return. "After that initial fight, the Indians were like, 'When's Bobby Gunn coming back? When is Bobby Gunn coming back?'" Feldman remembers. "It was a good night for them in the casino, and that's how I got them to discuss bare knuckle."

If any casino was up for gloveless battle, it was the Yavapai at Fort McDowell—a brave, independent tribe with a long history of defying government. The Yavapai Nation's motto is "Never Give Up." Always give back." But it might also be "Don't fuck with us." Despite their tiny size, the Yavapai are one of the most vehemently opposed tribes in Native Americans' most recent conflict with the federal government: the casino debate.

The Yavapai, who were once spread across ten million acres in central Arizona, were rounded up by US troops in the 1870s and relocated to an Apache reservation, many dying along the way, before settling in their present location, a former military installation in the Sonoran desert. For decades, the tribe ran a small bingo parlor and casino amid the saguaro cacti and cottonwoods, never making a stir, until one morning in 1992, when Linda A. Ak

A new federal regulation was at issue, which said that Indian reservations could only offer video gambling if the machines were sanctioned or already legal in the states around their land. Arizona's then-governor, Fife Symington, had prohibited the machines from casinos. But the Yavapai, not caring a whit for Symington's endorsement, had installed them anyhow, quickly making nearly 70 percent of their casino income from them—causing Arizona and the feds to retaliate.

On May 12, 1992, around daybreak, FBI agents attacked the Yavapai Casino, confiscating 349 video gambling machines and putting them onto vans for deportation. In response, tribal members organized to block the roadways with pickup trucks, vans, and front-end loaders. The stalemate generated a week of high-profile powwows and protests, reviving the national Native American sovereignty movement. "They will not do this to us," one tribal leader told the New York Times. "This time, they will not get away with it." After a stressful three weeks, Symington caved, ending the impasse and eventually signing a bill amending Arizona's gaming regulations, allowing the Yavapai to keep their machines. The Yavapai were the only tribe to take such a strong stance against the government on this matter, and they had prevailed. They still celebrate the protest anniversary as a national holiday.

In 2011, Feldman requested his business partner, Len Hayko, to speak with the Yavapai tribe in person about hosting Bad Boy's most daring event yet: the first legal bare-knuckle fight in the United States in over 120 years. It would be the spectacular climax to a "Bad Boy Fight Night" of boxing and MMA bouts, with the headline bare-knuckle brawl hopefully spawning a new sport and releasing Feldman from his bottom-tier roadhouse clashes and Extreme Midget Wrestling events. It was a massive risk, in complete violation of all US boxing laws. Despite the tribe's outlaw reputation, Feldman was confident they would refuse. Still, he and Hayko reasoned it couldn't harm to inquire. Hayko scheduled a meeting, expecting a simple dismissal—but instead received the shock of his life. He recalls his comments before the Yavapai tribal commission. "I was like, 'Yeah, we want to do a bare-knuckle battle.' And they were like, 'Aw, that's wonderful.' That was it. Nothing regarding regulations. "Nothing." He laughs. "So we started promoting it."

Feldman, barely believing his luck, scrambled for combatants. He eventually met Richard Stewart, a bald, flat-nosed 5'7" cruiserweight from Wilmington, Delaware, with a record of 14-9-2. Stewart, 35, was a bricklayer by trade who had lost his last five pro boxing contests, including three knockouts, and was forbidden from returning to the ring owing to health concerns. "When a fighter is knocked out consecutively like that, it's a good sign there are problems," Stewart's manager, Keith Stouffer, stated in 2011. "I have absolutely no interest in participating in this [bare-knuckle bout in Arizona]. It's quite dangerous."

But Stewart, who has his own underground reputation, recognized that fighting without gloves would be safer. More importantly, he was not going to turn down a payday. "Fighting ain't for the rich," he says. "This is a poor man's issue, bro. A lot of working-class men are just trying to pay their expenses." He sighs. "I was on vacation in Rehoboth Beach when I received that phone call. It was a last-minute fight. But bare knuckle is the way it is. "Money talks."

Stewart may not have been in peak condition, but everyone in the boxing world knew he could still throw—and in bare knuckle, all it takes is one punch. "He's a tough bastard," Gunn claims. "A rough fighter."

Finally, with everything in place but his big star, Feldman turned to Gunn. Gunn's sole ambition had been to become a world boxing champion, not bare knuckle. In fact, he had spent his entire career attempting to avoid the underground, even forbidding his son from entering it. And now he was being asked to glorify it, possibly even facing jail time, despite the fact that everyone knew he was already the underground's champion. Gunn was confused what to do when he received an unexpected call from Bert Sugar, the seventy-five-year-old, cigar-chomping, fedora-wearing inventor of the Ring magazine belt—boxing's highest prize and the championship Gunn had failed to seize from Adamek—who had heard about the potential match and wanted to speak with him.

"He said, 'If this fight is certified, you will be the first recognized bare-knuckle champion in a hundred and twenty-two years,'" Gunn tells me. "I told him, 'I already thought I was the bare-knuckle champ.' And he said, 'No, if you get this, then it's your stamp of legitimacy.'" For Gunn, this was the impetus he needed—the opportunity to become a legitimate world champion. He agreed to take the fight.

On a blistering 100-degree night in August 2011, Gunn faced Stewart of the Yavapai Nation tribe in the first sanctioned bare-knuckle boxing battle since 1889—a historic event that was under siege until the very end. After learning about the illicit contest, the Association of Boxing Commissions, the Arizona Attorney General's Office, and, according to Gunn's camp, even Arizona Senator John McCain—an avid traditionalist boxing fan who reportedly branded MMA "human cockfighting"—all attempted to shut it down.

"The casino had flooded the airwaves with TV commercials," Hayko says. "Bare-knuckle boxing is coming to Fort McDowell!'"Well, as soon as that was released, the boxing commission began calling, claiming that the event was not sanctioned. And the tribe responded, "We can do whatever we want." This is our land. "The Fort McDowell casino has approved it." Hayko pauses. "And, I mean, that's the law—it's a sovereign nation."

Unable to get traction, state officials appear to have resorted to a last-ditch effort. George Kokkalenios, a lawyer who occasionally works for Gunn, claims he was sleeping on his bed in a casino hotel room when the phone rang. It was McCain. "John McCain, God bless him, he's a war hero or whatever, but he called the hotel room, trying to shut it down," Kokkalenios tells me. "He asked, 'Give me someone higher up.' I replied, 'I don't think there is anyone higher up!'"

Even Gunn claims he chatted briefly with him. "I was on the phone with him for two seconds," Gunn explains. "He said, 'What I think you're doing is horrendous.' So I said, 'Not to be disrespectful, but I don't really have time for this.' And I hung up." (McCain's representatives did not return calls for comment.)

With the strain mounting, Gunn began to have second thoughts. "Everyone was going crazy," he recalls. "It was in the papers and on ESPN, and things were blown out of proportion. "I was getting really nervous." At 5:00 p.m., sitting in his hotel room in the last hours before the fight, Gunn says he received one last call, this time from an anonymous person threatening him with jail time if he went ahead with the fight. "They told me that when I left the casino property, I would get arrested by the local police," Gunn said. "I thought about it and then just said, 'Fuck it.'"

Gunn made up his mind. He'd come this far and wasn't backing down—nor were the Yavapai. "That reservation would have gone to war," Hayko explains. "The state was never going to shut that down." After effectively telling the government to go to hell, Gunn and the tribal elders finally made their way to the fight venue, a makeshift arena in a baking-hot parking lot—where, somehow, over 5,000 people had assembled to watch the spectacle.

"It was a big deal," Stewart remembers. "The place inside couldn't hold the people, so they did it in the parking lot." Neither the Yavapai nor anybody else had ever seen anything like this. Even ESPN touted the bout as "reviving a bygone, bare-knuckle era." Available for $10 as an online pay-per-view, the event had been described as a blood-soaked illegal brawl, with two officials present to ensure, according to one commentator, "the blood doesn't get too out of control."

Despite the hoopla, the battle was quite low-key. Feldman, surprised to receive tribal approval and concerned that they may alter their minds, pushed to complete the project in only a few weeks. The concert, sponsored by a nearby beer and wings joint named McDuffy's Sports Grill, included awful lighting, lousy music, and a ringside crew made up primarily of Feldman's friends and family. Feldman, wearing a red polo shirt and black jeans, declared the fight from the center of the ring. Shannon Ritch, a local bare-knuckle boxer, wore a headset and provided pay-per-view commentary alongside Feldman's 19-year-old son, Dave Jr., a college freshman. "The person we had couldn't make it, so I stepped in," Dave Jr. explains. "I was announcing local high school football games at the time."

Even the battle, which was advertised as a hazardous criminal clash, fell short of expectations. Toeing a fine line, Feldman was attempting to give an extreme event while also ensuring that no one was seriously injured, which could have generated a public reaction and effectively terminated his sport. To be safe, he confined the rounds to 90 seconds apiece, with a one-minute pause in between, and hired two referees to oversee the match at the same time.

Gunn, an underground fighter used to no rules or time constraints, was out of sync from the outset. Wearing black trunks with a Star of David and the words "Give God the Glory," he circled the ring, waiting and watching. Stewart, plainly out of shape, feinted and danced, but punched sparingly. "I'd never been on that side of the Mississippi," he tells me. "It was like an oven." The slow action attracted groans from the audience, who quickly identified the entire event as a sanitized version of what everyone had come to see: a bare-knuckle street fight.

"It's not the big bloodbath everybody thought it was going to be," Ritch said from the commentator's booth.

Gunn struggled through the first two rounds, clearly out of his comfort zone, until the third round's bell rang—and he suddenly came alive. After finally getting a read on his opponent, Gunn unleashed, flooring Stewart with a combo to the body and a tap on the chin. Stewart attempted to stand, fell, and then rose again, wobbling and bleeding from a terrible gash beneath his left eye. Without hesitation, Gunn moved to his stumbling opponent, almost gently lifted his hands away from his face as if brushing aside a lock of hair, and fired a crushing haymaker directly to Stewart's cut eye, flooring him as Feldman waved his arms, signaling the end of the contest.

"And the struggle is finished!" Feldman Jr. yelled as a remix of Black Sabbath's "Ironman" played over the ceiling speakers. "Bobby Gunn, overhand right!" ...There is history, ladies and gentlemen!"

Gunn and Feldman estimated only 50,000 people to live-stream the internet event, which would generate approximately $500,000. Instead, more than a million people attempted to watch, disrupting the fight's payment system and, with it, any possibility of a long-awaited paycheck. "We made very little," Feldman will simply reply now, still outraged by the incident.

Nonetheless, it provided all the proof they needed that bare-knuckle fighting was ready for the public. Within hours, Gunn's Facebook page was inundated with views, and his Twitter followers quickly grew to over 40,000. Finally, he had taken a significant step toward the stardom that had escaped him throughout his life.

CHAPTER 12
FIGHTING IN THE SHADOWS

*A*fter Gunn's bare-knuckle fights became viral, a strange thing happened: pro boxing promoters became interested in him again, urging him to return to the ring.

In February 2012, barely two months after dropping Jackson in a warehouse, Gunn announced his first professional boxing battle in nearly three years. It would be a heavyweight title fight against former three-division world champion James "Lights Out" Toney at the Landers Center, an 8,400-seat venue located twenty miles south of Memphis. "James Toney to rumble with bare knuckle champ Bobby Gunn," the headlines read.

At the February news conference, Toney, a former world number-one boxer with a 77-7-3 record who was now on a senior tour, made a point of mentioning Gunn's criminal character. "I don't get paid to fight in the street," Toney, 43, remarked from the stage. "You gypsy pig." 2

Gunn, dressed in a black tracksuit, rushed the former champion. "Gypsy pig?" Gunn yelled. "I'm a gypsy fighter! We'll go out onto the street right now!"

Gunn intended it. In preparation for his battle, Gunn devoted himself to round-the-clock training at Ike's gym in Paterson, New Jersey, sparring anytime he wasn't pouring asphalt or driving his daughter to school. But no matter how hard Gunn tried, he was unable to escape the underground. Gunn took on a bare-knuckle battle staged by the Irish gang just three weeks before his pro boxing contest against Toney, since he was broke and needed money to fund the expenditures of his preparation.

"I went down to Hell's Kitchen late at night, walked through the bar, down through a door in the floor, and fought," Gunn tells me. "Only the elite was allowed in." The Irish were pitting Gunn against a fighter brought in by the Italian mafia—the main event in an evening of gambling and drinking between the two criminal groups. Gunn, who was in peak physical condition as a result of his training, dispatched his opponent quickly. "They brought in some big Italian guy, a little soft in the midsection," Gunn tells me. "I fought him with a double left hook, split his eye right open, and he went down." Gunn felt the fight was over. However, after forty seconds, the Italian immediately sprang off the floor, eager to battle again. "The Irish started freaking out," Gunn explains. "It's Bobby Gunn! Fucking good! Fuck him, uuup! '" Gunn shrugged. "So I come on again, and we rock and roll." Gunn quickly knocked him out, winning the fight and taking home $10,000. But he didn't get away unscathed—he fractured his hand on the man's head. "I'd hurt my hand," Gunn admits. "It was fucked up, swollen."

Despite his injury, Gunn returned to the ring two days later. After weigh-ins and press activities at a smoky, mildewed casino on the Mississippi River, Gunn faced Toney in front of four hundred beer-drinking locals at the virtually empty Landers Center. The non televised event was a thunderous thud. Gunn landed some hard jabs early on, but his decision to fight for the money with a fractured right hand—as he had done so many times in the past—proved fatal, shattering his fist. Toney, despite weighing 248 pounds, proceeded to pick the bare-knuckle champion apart. After battling through five rounds, Gunn's corner, led by Feldman, gave up. What's the reason? A fractured hand. "I'm gonna get it x-rayed," Gunn remarked later, his eyes battered, his face bleeding, and his dreams wrecked once more. "I lost big."

For the next few years, Gunn virtually completely stopped boxing. Instead, he proceeded to play a risky new game, fighting in underground matches (some taped, most not) and attempting to establish it as a new sport—all while avoiding Greg Sirb, executive director of the Pennsylvania State Athletic Commission, at all times. "That fucking Greg Sirb," Gunn admits, shaking his head even now. "He tortured me."

Gunn's battle with Sirb began in Arizona in 2011. During the buildup to the battle, news focused on federal commissioners and Arizona lawmakers attempting to end the bare-knuckle combat. But it was Sirb, a lesser-known but ambitious state commissioner three thousand miles away, who helped start the trouble.

According to the notes of a national meeting of the Association of Boxing Commissioners, held just days before the bout, Sirb gave a lecture on "bare-knuckle fighting" in which he "urged all 14 tribal members of the ABC to send the Fort McDowell Tribe a letter noting that such activity contravenes the laws and regulations attendant to professional boxing." Then, according to Gunn, Feldman, and others involved with the event, Sirb began prodding various politicians. Following the overwhelming backlash against the fight, the Fort McDowell representatives reportedly wrote their apology not to Tim Lueckenhoff, then president of the ABC, but to his vice president, Sirb. On the surface, it appears unlikely that a Pennsylvania state athletic commissioner would try to stop a bare-knuckle fight in Arizona—and then spend the next few years trying to bring down Gunn and destroy the sport entirely. But, as Gunn and Feldman quickly discovered, Sirb lived and breathed boxing and would go to any length to preserve it from possible dangers.

Sirb, the main commissioner against bare knuckle fighting, is the lone authority in Pennsylvania fight sports, overseeing careers, licenses, and permits in the nearly $1 million annual state industry, and he runs his jurisdiction with the hard-ass discipline of a drill sergeant. "I'm probably one of the only commissioners who grew up boxing and wrestling," he admits. "I'm not some punk-ass political appointee."

Sirb, a former wrestling coach who grew up in Sharon, Pennsylvania, is a short man with a high forehead and dark circles under his eyes—the result of crisscrossing the state since 1990 to oversee its sixty-odd annual boxing, wrestling, MMA, and kickboxing events. At ringside, he is a staple, his tucked-in polo shirt buttoned to the chin, his back ramrod straight, and his face a fierce don't-fuck-with-me expression. Sirb, an old-school boxer, helped build Pennsylvania into a pugilistic powerhouse with over 400 licensed boxers, the third highest number of boxing events in the US, and one of the highest revenues in the country, earning him accolades from US Olympic boxing associations and a seat on the Governor's Council on Physical Fitness and Sports. In 1997, he even testified before Congress in an effort to create a pension system for pro boxers and protect them from explosions.

Safeguarding fighters is a difficult job, and Sirb takes it seriously, despite his harsh exterior, which occasionally conceals the reality that it keeps him awake at night. "My job is a very tricky balance," explains the employee. "Boxing poses the greatest danger for the dollar when compared to football, drag racing, and rodeo. "You just can't whitewash it." He pauses. "I believe it is a legitimate, beautiful sport. If you grew up in the inner city like I did, you're drawn to these physical conflicts. I love it. But the drive home after a fight is tough. I hope the boy who was beaten up is not hurt. I hope you don't get a call at 2 a.m. from the kid's trainer, mother, or father informing you that he was taken to the hospital. We had one death. And, you know, it is difficult to discuss. That is still with me. "It will never leave."

Sirb regards himself as the sole protector of boxing. However, in his efforts to protect it, he has earned another reputation among some fighters and promoters—for running his commission like a dictatorship, bullying underlings, waging vendettas, and, most damningly, supporting only boxing while working to prevent new fight sports from entering Pennsylvania, one of the last states in the country to sanction MMA. Look up his name, and a slew of headlines appear: "Remove Abusive PA Athletic Commission Exec Dir. Greg Sirb From Office." "I Was Assaulted by Pennsylvania Commissioner Greg Sirb." "Greg Sirb is the devil!"

The last one makes Sirb laugh. "I love MMA," he says. "Guys undoubtedly claim we're too strict, since they came here and got their ass beaten." But there is one rumor Sirb will confirm: bare-knuckle boxing will not make its debut in Pennsylvania—as he puts it, "P. A."—any time soon. "No, I'm not supportive," he says. "Look, due to the popularity of MMA, which everyone said was impossible, I have to keep an open mind. But I don't believe there is enough research on bare-knuckle fighting to draw any conclusions about its safety." He stops. "Dave is always pushing the envelope, and it's my job as commissioner to rein him in—'That's not going to happen.'"

Sirb has long been at odds with the Feldman family, a group of fight organizers infamous for breaking the law. "Both brothers are hustlers," he explains. "Always looking for something new: the next kid, the next champ, the next sport." The athletic commissioner respects Marty, the "tough and mean old man." ..In 2010, however, he filed criminal charges against Damon, Feldman's older brother, a celebrity boxing promoter who sets D-list celebs (José Canseco, Danny Bonaduce, Michael Lohan) against each other for manipulating fights.

Around the same time, Feldman claims Sirb pursued him, nearly damaging his career by attempting to shut down his first pro MMA event, an Xtreme Fight Event at the now-defunct Tri-State Sports Complex in Aston, just hours before it was about to begin—all over a personal vendetta. "He didn't like my brother, so he tried to take it out on me," Feldman explains. "I had every dollar from that show. So I told Greg, "Everyone calls you a Napoleon motherfucker, and I stand up for you." I work my tail off. Show me respect!'And he apologized for letting me perform the show." (Sirb claims this did not occur.)

But none of the battles compared to the war that erupted over bare-knuckle boxing. According to Feldman, the 2011 bout in Arizona enraged the commissioner, giving the impression that he couldn't control a promoter from his own state. Then, after the Ernest Jackson bare-knuckle fight went viral, Gunn and Feldman claim Sirb threatened to take away their boxing licenses, prompting an investigation into whether they were holding underground fights in Pennsylvania. (Sirb confirms the probe but denies issuing threats.) For years, Sirb played cat-and-mouse with Gunn and Feldman, hoping to catch them in the underground.

While the two did not work together on every bare-knuckle battle for Gunn—"Remember, I brought him into my world," Gunn says—Feldman oversaw enough to gain a taste for the sport, bringing in boxers and MMA fighters while attempting to devise a strategy for establishing it as a legitimate company. "The first one I ever did, I was nervous that we were gonna get jammed up by the cops," Feldman tells me. "When we left, I was like, 'Wow, that was fucking incredible. "We need to video this and sell it on the internet."

Making things even more perilous, Gunn and Feldman continued to work together on pro boxing events, which meant they would occasionally see Sirb on the same day as an underground fight. Feldman once went from a bare-knuckle battle to a pro boxing contest, where the Pennsylvania commissioner instantly tried to arrest him based on a tip he had received about a warehouse fight. "He knew I was doing it but could never prove it," Feldman explains. "He'd say, 'I'm going to bring you in front of the board for the bare-knuckle thing,' and I'd say, 'What are you talking about? I was sleeping at home.Feldman laughs. "I'd fuck with him about bare knuckle: 'You better make sure no one gets killed in that shit.'" 14

After years of escaping Sirb, Gunn and Feldman decided to stage their most brazen underground match yet: a fight captured by 60 Minutes Sports. In order to generate groundbreaking publicity and, hopefully, drive bare knuckle to public acceptance, they teamed up with Danny Provenzano, a felon and bare-knuckle promoter with experience in another world: show business.

In 2003, right before going to jail, Provenzano released a self-penned, self-directed mob flick, This Thing of Ours, featuring James Caan, which included a scene mirroring one of the forty-four indictments that had been leveled against him—that he once ordered a thieving employee's thumb to be smashed with a hammer. And now Provenzano was launching his own media company, Genco.TV, named after the olive oil company that Vito Corleone uses as a business front in The According to Gunn, Provenzano was the one who contacted 60 Minutes and invited them to film his match. So Gunn decided to do something previously unthinkable: throw a light on the subterranean.

On a Saturday night in March 2014, Gunn walked through snow on trash-strewn sidewalks to an auto-body shop in a big northeastern city. Wearing a gray hoodie and baseball cap, he walked up a flight of stairs and entered a vast cavernous room, fitting in with the group of fifty. On the concrete floor, two parallel strips of tape had been put, with the undercard fighters squaring off with their toes to the lines and encircled by cameras. As the opening round began, Gunn removed his hoodie and went through his pre-fight routine, working his hands, stretching his neck, and attempting to clear his thoughts.

Inviting the cameras had been dangerous. Nonetheless, Gunn felt compelled to take action. In the coming weeks, his son, Bobby Jr., would make his professional boxing debut, against a thirty-year-old middleweight with a 0-3 record at a Boys and Girls Club in Annandale, Virginia. Although Bobby Jr. was only seventeen, he had already established a 25-2 record as an amateur and was practically certain of winning, prompting Gunn to consider the long term. Pro boxing handlers began to sweep in, offering the youngster contracts, and Gunn, ever protective, turned them all down. Some questioned whether Gunn was being overly cautious, preventing Bobby Jr. from realizing his potential. But Gunn was insistent. He was attempting to lay a foundation for his son that he had never enjoyed, and he would personally oversee Bobby Jr.'s pro boxing career until he was ready to delegate it to someone else.

The only thing Gunn needed was more money—and perhaps taping today's match would help with that, resulting in another massive bare-knuckle fight and a payoff. "Nobody will have my boy," Gunn declares. "I'm bringing him up the way I should have been brought up myself—by giving him everything I've never had."

With the final undercard match completed, Gunn faced his opponent, a thirty-five-year-old pro heavyweight boxer known as "George Streeter." Standing a few feet apart, Gunn and Streeter—both about 200 pounds, both dressed in muscle shirts and jeans, both long-time underground vets—sized each other up. "All right, let's do this," Provenzano screamed, clapping his fists. "Let's fight!"

Almost immediately, Gunn struck Streeter with a left jab to the nose. But Streeter, a seasoned fighter with a claimed 33-6 bare-knuckle record, remained unfazed, countering with jabs to the torso. For the following two minutes, the couple walked around the concrete floor, exchanging blows and avoiding feints. Finally, after nearly a minute of punching little and waiting, Gunn saw an opening. Like a sniper, he unleashed a pinpoint left hook to Streeter's right eye, sending the pro heavyweight to the knees, clutching his face, and the audience erupting. Gunn walked away before Streeter even touched the ground, knowing the fight was done. "He's out," Provenzano said. "That's it."

That night, Gunn left with an estimated $40,000, allowing him to properly train Bobby Jr. and guide him to a 5-0 pro boxing record—a sensational start with four knockouts and a world youth title. "By the time this boy is twenty-one, he'll be fighting for a world middleweight title," Gunn informed me months later. "From my mouth to God's ears, I hope it happens that way."

The cost of Gunn's win, however, had been high. When it premiered, the 60 Minutes Sports part was a murky thirteen-minute feature that highlighted the underground and included interviews with Provenzano, Gunn, and an ex-con known as Johnny "Knuckles." The host declared that the show had recorded "the bloody sport in its rawest form."

After it aired, Sirb stepped up his efforts. Gunn would never again participate in a sanctioned bare-knuckle bout. In fact, he claims the TV spot harmed his chances of another quality battle, with the show's representation of the underground putting all potential bare-knuckle venues at arm's length, none wanting to be linked with the sport. To avoid harassment and possibly punishment by Sirb, Gunn's accomplice, Feldman, did not renew his Pennsylvania promoter's license. Joey Eye, the Philadelphia cut man who attended the underground match, claims that Sirb finally banned him in six states, costing him thousands of dollars in legal fees and keeping him out of work for nearly a year. "He had his people haul me out of a locker room at a pro boxing match and then he called me up screaming," Eye tells me. "He is a total Napoleon!" ("That's his version of things," Sirb comments on the situation.)

Gunn would fight seldom over the next three years. "I was scared," he admits. "We were under the gun."

CHAPTER 13
IN THE WILD WEST

*G*unn sleeps on a bed around midnight, having suffered a crushing defeat. He is exhausted and bloodied, and he does not want to leave his hotel room at the Westin Hotel, which is near to the Chase Center boxing stadium. However, he needs to take Max outside one last time, so he decides to go ahead and check on his son. Bobby Jr., a normally quiet child, was enraged at his father's defeat, storming into the center of the ring and screaming at Jones, "You never got him down!" You never brought him down!" Gunn, completely astonished, had stepped between his son and Jones, unsure of what to expect. But Jones, knowing something about a son's love for his father, simply looked at the boy, the cameras swirling around them, and consented. "No, I didn't," Jones replied. "He's a tough motherfucker," the teenager said.

Gunn, his eyes blacked, nose bruised, and a deep cut running like a knife scar down his right cheek, gets out of bed, puts on a black tracksuit, and picks Max up into his arms. He's forty-three and feels sixty-three, and he doesn't want to leave this room. But he needs to check on his son and knows precisely where he will be: the bar. For nights on end, the bar at the Westin has been a Traveler gathering place, with various Scottish, Irish, and English clans gathering to put aside their differences, sing songs, and drink until someone irritates someone else and the violence continues all over again. "Are you here for boxing?" A housekeeper asks me in the hotel elevator one morning. "I got here at six in the morning and they were still cleaning up the lobby from the fight last night."

Gunn steps out of the elevator, Max tucked under his arm, and heads inside the busy pub. It's a sweaty sea of techno music, clinking cocktails, and loud talk, with everyone on a high from the battle.

After wading through numerous Travelers eager to shake his hand or take a photo, Gunn discovers Bobby Jr., who does not drink but is socializing with friends. The boy's hoodie is still stained with blood from the ring incident, but he appears to be happy now, so Gunn chooses to sit and enjoy the chat. He orders some water. When he blows into a Kleenex, he creates a bloody mess. However, the fighter remains cool. A fresh resolution and a sorrowful acceptance. "I'm done with boxing," Gunn states, shaking his head. "I think Roy was taking it easy on me."

Gunn had already left the ring when Feldman took the microphone and announced to the sold-out audience and the rest of the globe that bare-knuckle boxing would return this year. And, of course, that meant one thing: Gunn, the aging marquee star, would take to the canvas for the final time. He shook his head, appearing older. His father would continue to brawl until he could no longer stand, and now his own son had attempted to rough up a future Hall of Famer on a national pay-per-view broadcast. Bare-knuckle boxing was simply in his blood. And if he couldn't go out as a champion in the ring, he'd at least do so without gloves. There has to be one last struggle.

"I've still got it," Gunn says. "I am still the best out there. None of these other guys can fight Roy. This year, I'm defending my title—I put bare-knuckle boxing on the map.

Gunn is relaxing, caressing Max, and contemplating his next move when he receives word that three Irish Travelers are seeking for him. Standing, Gunn approaches the men. They are from Ireland, are unfamiliar to the community, and appear inebriated, aggressive, and eager to start something. "Hey," one of them says to Gunn, moving in too close and pressing a smartphone on his face. "My sister wants to say hello."

Gunn does not notice the empty beer bottle in the man's hand or his attempt to swing it at his face. But his son does. Bobby Jr. grabs the man and pushes him away, punching him as the throng swarms. Gunn's son is battling with abandon, as if something has been unleashed within him, when one of the other two guys intervenes to take a cheap hit at the child.

Wrong move.

Gunn swivels, his bloodshot eyes coming into focus, and grabs the man. Smooth as a greased piston, he slips two fingers into the man's nostrils and pulls up and up and up, hearing a crunch, then a pop of severed cartilage, and finally seeing as the tip of the nose rips completely apart.

The third man runs away.

Gunn is alone in a ring, shadowboxing, sweating, and breathing heavily. "Huh! He growls, throws three left jabs, ducks an imaginary attacker, and advances. "Ha! " he exclaims, rotating on his good leg and repeating the motion. Bobby Jr. is still staring at his smartphone at ringside. Outside, Gunn's French bulldog, Max, is sleeping in the vehicle. On this Saturday morning in July 2017, in a south Philadelphia arena, the only person paying attention to the bare-knuckle champion is a heavily tattooed young fighter from Rahway, New Jersey, a part-time pizza delivery guy who has come here with dozens of other fighters for one reason: to meet Gunn and, hopefully, follow in his footsteps. "This guy's a legend," the boy says, looking up at Gunn. "You are a warrior!"

Gunn shook his hands, rolled his neck, and stepped out of the ring. He is not here to compete—he is dressed in a black baseball cap, black polo shirt, and jeans—and has entered the ring only out of habit, an almost bodily desire to tread the canvas whenever he sees it. No, Gunn is here for a much more important cause, one he never expected: to help launch the Bare Knuckle Fighting Championship, a new professional combat league that will premiere in the coming months.

Today, thirty combatants from across the United States will compete for a limited number of league spots, all wearing black jerseys with gold fists on the front and numbers on the backs. Under Gunn and Feldman's watchful eyes, the prospects will go through a series of tests—sparring with pads, working bags, and measuring their strength against a "punch meter"—all in an effort to secure a spot on the league's first bare-knuckle event, a pay-per-view match that Gunn will headline in Kansas in the coming months. Today's tryout, orchestrated by Feldman, from the officials to the clothes to the five-man crew filming everything for a potential reality show, feels full of promise—a new venture on the verge of success.

Not that Gunn feels any of it.

"I'm dead broke," he admits, smiling tightly as another young warrior approaches for a photo. "A quick fight for ten grand sure would be good about now."

Gunn, in possibly the biggest irony of his life, is about to leave the underground, but all he can think about is going back into it. "I used to just take one on when I needed money," he says, looking at the cameras and promoters. "But I can't do stupid stuff anymore. "There is just too much at stake."

If things continue as they are, Gunn will die. Last night, after a week of paving roads and painting barns in distant upstate New York, he slept in his vehicle by the side of the highway, waking up to cicadas and sweat to drive the three hundred miles south for the audition. As usual, he has been working extra hours to make ends meet—and he is barely getting by. In two weeks, Gunn must pay $3,000 to renew his truck's professional tags and licenses. And then there's the looming rent payment, the $10,000 in credit card debt, and, God help him, Charlene's private school tuition for the autumn, which is just around the horizon. Gunn rubs his face and pulls out his smartphone to look at a family photo from the recent Cancún trip, everyone smiling in similar Hawaiian shirts. "I don't know where I'm going to get the money," he tells me. "Things are getting desperate."

Unable to fight in the subterranean, Gunn has decided to return to the boxing ring. In a week, he will face Gilberto Domingos, a thirty-one-year-old Brazilian heavyweight with a 22-8 record, for $2,500 in a makeshift ring outside a Harley-Davidson showroom in Huntington, West Virginia. It's a long way from Caesar's Palace—along with Gunn's latest battle against Roy Jones—and the bout's desperation is only heightened by Gunn's current sloppy training routine. Unable to hit the gym at Ike's, he has been practicing for the match by standing on the bed of his truck and doing one-arm rows with fifty-five-pound buckets of asphalt sealer. "It weighs a lot," Gunn states. "But it's still not proper training."

Gunn sighs as he surveys the arena, which is primarily filled with young combatants who have memorized his YouTube fights. In addition to the twenty-eight-year-old pizza-delivery brawler, there is John Hernholm, twenty-nine, a gigantic 6'6", 350-pound bouncer from Knoxville, Tennessee, who recently gained notoriety for knocking out an intoxicated hooligan at a club. The resultant smartphone video garnered 23 million views, prompting him to travel the ten hours here in quest of a new job. Next to him is Sam Shewmaker, a thirty-three-year-old 6'3", 250-pound construction worker from Kansas City, Missouri, who flew here with his trainer, a seventy-two-year-old junkyard owner, in the hopes of providing a better life for his three children. "I got an offer to fight from a biker gang last month," Shewmaker says while posing for a photo with Gunn. "Human nature is brutal."

The contenders include two warriors who had previously fallen to Gunn in the underground. Mike Liberto, a thirty-three-year-old steelworker and MMA fighter, faced Gunn in a warehouse bout. "Bobby's punch angles come from nowhere," he claims. "He split my head wide open."

And Jim McClendon, the former marine who fought Gunn in a New Jersey auto-body shop in 2015, claims that losing to the champ boosted his reputation in the underground, resulting in more bare-knuckle fights and money toward his goal of purchasing a home. "I'm just trying to fight my way into a home," he tells me. "I see opportunity in this."

Gunn smiles at everyone and poses for photos. "Keep doing what you're doing," he advises. "In order to win in life you have to go through things you wouldn't wish on your worst enemy."

Gunn taps a ringside bell ten times with a hammer and says a prayer before the match begins. The thirty prospective fighters get to work, and the arena rapidly becomes a whirlpool of punches, swinging bags, and the howling exertions of warriors striking the "punch meter," a force plate placed to a wall to measure strength. "Total waste of time," says Dom, Gunn's veteran trainer, crossing his arms over his abdomen and staring at the punch meter. "As if it matters how hard you can hit someone with bare knuckles. It's all about perfection.

A man wearing a fedora disagrees. "This is fantastic," says Art Davie, creator of the UFC. "We used a punch meter at UFC One. It simply looks nice. "Marketing is everything."

Perhaps the most insane aspect of Gunn's plan to change his life by making bare knuckle boxing a global professional sport is that it isn't so crazy. Davie, 70, has done it before. At first impression, Brooklyn-born Davie looks like a carnival hustler, dressed in a houndstooth jacket and brandishing an unlit Cuban cigar the size of a baton. You'll think, "There's no way this guy is on level." However,

Davie is responsible for one of contemporary sports' greatest triumphs, a massive magic trick that helped transform MMA from a fringe outlaw competition to a mainstream sport and a $12 billion global phenomenon. "Art Davie is here," Gunn replies, shaking his head in surprise. "This is going to explode!"

Gunn should be thrilled. Davie, who is here as an adviser, understands every method for pulling this off. In 1993, while working as an adman in Los Angeles, he fell into the fight business after attempting to persuade a client, Tecate beer, to sponsor a kickboxing event. Realizing there was no real promotion for martial arts exhibitions, Davie thought back to a fight he had heard about as a marine in Vietnam, between a wrestler and a boxer in a Bangkok bar. He began dreaming up a new sport that would put different styles of fighters against each other, and enlisted Rorion Gracie, a Brazilian jiu jitsu expert, and John Milius, the cigar-chomping, gun-loving Hollywood screenwriter of Dirty Harry, Apocalypse Now, and Conan the Barbarian, to Borrowing heavily from the ancient Greek sport Pankration—a contest in which everything except biting, eye gouging, and attacking genitals was permitted—the three men created the Ultimate Fighting Championship, a bloody, showy bare-knuckle no-holds-barred tournament that pitted combatants from all disciplines against one another.

Surprisingly, they secured a TV agreement with Bob Meyrowitz, a Manhattan-based entertainment mogul who had earned a fortune arranging pay-per-view concerts for bands ranging from Ozzy Osbourne to the New Kids on the Block. Meyrowitz, a former boxer, believed that the combat scene was due for a shakeup. "Everyone says that music is the international language, but it's not true," he said at the time. "With the exception of a few mega-acts, music is best described as regional. But everywhere I go, I see fighting. Fighting is the international language. ..Everyone gets it."

Twenty years later, after defeating politicians and commentators who labeled the gory sport as the death of civilization, the UFC was sold for $4.2 billion to an international company that included William Morris Endeavor, the Kraft company, and Dalian Wanda, the world's largest private property developer. The UFC was valued at $12.1 billion in 2023. Although Davie sold his stake in 1995 for $1 million, he went on to invest in other ventures and now believes bare knuckle boxing might be the next UFC event. "This could make a billion bucks," he adds as he watches the combatants during the tryout. "Dave's got the chutzpah, and Bobby is the greatest exponent of the sport."

Davie feels that the key to Gunn and Feldman's success is to sell the savagery of bare-knuckle fighting to a jaded millennial audience, introducing them to a new sport as raw, nasty, and captivating as the streets. It's how Davie succeeded with the UFC, by attracting his brightest talents from the meanest corners of the underground. "I had bare-knuckle fighters in all of my first ten UFC matches," he recalls, watching a contestant wreak havoc on his opponent. "My biggest star back then was Tank Abbott, and I discovered him in a parking lot in Escondido, fighting for a thousand bucks. He annihilated this big Samoan boy from Orange County, putting him to the ground, kicking him in the head, and then going to the guy's entourage and saying, 'That was extra.'" Davie grins. "I said, 'I love this guy!'"

Like Gunn and Feldman, Davie looked everywhere for his first UFC combatants, including signing a swastika-tattooed enforcer from an Amsterdam brothel. "Gerard Gordeau was an ice-cold Dutchman," Davie explains. "John Milius said he had the soul of a CIA assassin." According to Davie, Gordeau, a world champion kickboxer, was moonlighting as an underworld tough when Davie learned about him through a gym manager and encouraged him to fight in UFC One in 1993. "Gordeau handled all the muscle jobs for the brothel and rave-club owners," Davie tells me. "He had a .32 pistol in his back pocket, and a razor in his sock—I knew he'd be a real tough guy."

Gordeau, a slender, pale 6'5" boxer weighing 216 pounds and sporting a buzz cut and wispy goatee, did not appear tough at first impression. In reality, it appeared that he would be crushed by his opponent, Teila Tuli, a 6'2" 420-pound sumo wrestler from Honolulu. But Gordeau's eyes—dark, deep-set, unflinching—told a different narrative. Less than thirty seconds into the first match at UFC One in Denver, Gordeau kicked Tuli with a roundhouse to the teeth, followed by a right jab to the eye, exploding the sumo wrestler's socket and sending his teeth flying out over the audience, including the heads of the Gold's Gym sponsors in the front row. (They never sponsored another match.) The fight lasted 26 seconds.

Davie, pleased with the vibe, went backstage to check on Gordeau, who was smoking a cigarette while a doctor used tweezers to remove shards of tooth from his foot. "I asked if he was okay, and he just said what he always said," Davie recalled. "'No problem, Art Davie.'" Almost everyone else had major issues with it. Sports Illustrated had sent a reporter to cover the event, but the editors, horrified by the brutality, opted not to publish the story. "Fighting is not what we thought it was," observed a shell-shocked broadcaster at the event.

Davie was ultimately proven correct: the UFC's extreme violence and speed quickly made it one of the world's most popular sports. However, the issue remained: might bare knuckles catch on in the same way?

Gunn observes the fighters. "He's a wrassler," Gunn remarks, dismissing a young man's MMA stance in the ring. "Look how he squares up. "He can only deliver one punch at a time."

Gunn has little interest in mixed martial arts. But he respects Davie and what he has done for the UFC, and he hopes his predictions about bare knuckle will come true. If the underground sport is ever going to take off, now is the time. In England, where it is legal, bare knuckle has grown in recent years, even being staged at one of the country's most prestigious venues, the O2 Arena in London, in June. And now, as it gains traction in the United States, Gunn has seen the underground sport attract an increasing number of MMA fighters, young men used to getting kneed in the face and less bothered by the blood and broken bones that come with bare-fisted shots.

Gunn would like to see more young boxers into the sport, but thanks to Davie, all the kids are drawn to UFC superstars like Ronda Rousey, Conor McGregor, and Randy Couture and want to fight MMA. If Davie can do it for bare knuckles, Gunn is willing to disregard his own biases. "It really means something that he's here," Gunn adds, glancing at the fedora-wearing entrepreneur, who is standing next to a Kansas Athletic Commission representative. "He wouldn't be here else, right?"

Gunn feels optimistic about the Kansas match. However, he has come close to realizing his aspirations. Several years ago, he discussed fighting Davie's former UFC star Tank Abbott in a high-profile bare-knuckle bout. But that about, like every sanctioned bare-knuckle fight Gunn has attempted since his 2011 match in Arizona—from a face-off against Kimbo Slice to his most recent bid against Shannon Ritch—failed. Now Kansas says it is interested in him fighting in a major pay-per-view event, which is expected to take place in the fall.

Davie is on board. Sean Wheelock, a member of the Kansas Athletic Commission, is present for the tryouts. Even Gunn's former nemesis, Pennsylvania commissioner Greg Sirb, has changed his mind and is now willing to talk about a state-sponsored event.

"I would never have guessed he would call in a million years," Feldman adds, suggesting that the commissioner does not want to miss out on bare-knuckle after being so late in sanctioning MMA. "If he wants to do it, then there's nobody I can't convince."

But Gunn is still unsure. If Kansas is staging the fight, why hasn't a date been set yet? Gunn sneaks out early, hoping to make some headlines and inspire the heartland state to action. He drives back home to prepare for his match. A week later, in West Virginia, he knocks out Domingos, the Brazilian heavyweight with a 22-8 record, in under four minutes, while the audience cries, "Finish him, finish him, finish him!" It is a fairly one-sided encounter, the ending Gunn always hoped for in his bouts with world champions—victories that never materialized. But with this seemingly regular victory in the heart of coal country, Gunn accomplished something even more significant. Gunn just won the Canadian Professional Boxing Council International title—an unimportant belt, but a belt nonetheless—making him the only boxer in US history since John L. Sullivan to hold heavyweight titles in both pro boxing and bare knuckle.

Gunn created history. And now Kansas will undoubtedly fall into place, allowing him to finally finish his $100,000 fight against Ritch—the last big bare-knuckle match of his career.

"It felt great to get the W," Gunn adds, beaming among the glistening Harleys. "The Gunslinger is back."

CHAPTER 14
PASSING THE TORCH

*S*tanding on the outside edge of the boxing ring, Gunn grips the ropes, his enormous hands white-knuckled, eyes shining with adrenaline as the surrounding audience screams in this smoke-stained run-down casino in New Cumberland, West Virginia. Bobby Jr. circles his opponent, an experienced forty-four-year-old welterweight named Mike Miranda, who has a 44-6 record. It's the second round of this September 2017 headlining pro boxing battle at the Mountaineer Casino Ballroom, and Bobby Jr.—only twenty years old and 8-0—is looking for an upset.

Miranda, his opponent, is a seasoned professional with forty proven knockouts, several world title battles, and, despite his age, a right hook that can drop an ox. In reality, when Bobby Jr. was first offered the opportunity to compete for the World Boxing Council FECARBOX super-middleweight title, his manager and trainer, Gunn, declined. "I turned it down immediately," Gunn adds. "This was a hardened, seasoned bum."

However, after watching Miranda's battles on YouTube, Gunn realized that the veteran had a blind spot. "I saw something," Gunn recalls. "The guy is a southpaw. When he battled for his previous world title, he was dropped with a left punch to the body—and Bobby enjoys that left hook because he is a winger."

Now, as he watches his son fight under the lights, Gunn experiences an unusual sensation: nervousness. The Mountaineer Casino may be a faded resort in a former mining town in the Appalachian mountains, but the belt is real, providing Bobby Jr. with the opportunity to finally put his lifetime of lessons to use and carry on his ancestral legacy. Gunn has been preparing his kid for this moment since he was a child, making him run with five-gallon buckets of asphalt sealant during roadside jobs and having him go to Ike's every day to work the bags and spar. Now it's time for Bobby Jr. to take the initiative. Now it's time for him to do something no other member of the Gunn family has ever done: become a world champion boxer at the age of twenty—and his father can't bear to watch. "My heart is in my throat," Gunn admits, wiping his face. "My nerves are totally shot."

His wife, Rose, is praying at church and refuses to mention her son's entry into the ring. "It makes Mommy upset when my brother gets hit with a black eye," eight-year-old Charlene says at one point. "It makes me upset too."

Gunn wills himself to be confident as he stands on the ring's edge, the air smelling of bloodthirst and cheap well drinks. If nothing else, he knows he has given his son one guaranteed strategy: he can predict how an aging boxer will strike. "An old pro will squat down, hoping to get a young buck to start swinging wildly," according to Gunn. "Then he'll catch him on the chin." He grins. "Basically, I told Bobby to watch out for what I would do to him."

Bap!

Gunn flinches when Bobby Jr. takes a hit. "Come on, son!" he cries, beating his palms into the canvas, the gold "Bobby Jr." writing on his black T-shirt glaring under the lights. "Give him the punch!"

Bobby Jr. takes a step forward toward his opponent in the ring. Bobby Jr., dressed in black shoes, black socks, and black trunks with his name engraved in gold lettering across the front waistband, resembles his father's chiseled, slender figure. Bobby Jr.'s typical peaceful manner is gone. The slouched position is gone. He, like his father, has evolved into a different animal in the ring, a powerhouse of stone-eyed rage and discipline with one goal in mind: to destroy

Miranda and claim his prize. "In the ring, the beast comes out," Bobby Jr. later explains. "The adrenaline simply takes over. "I know what I want and what I'll get."

Miranda fires a jab in the second round, leaving his left side vulnerable to attack—and Bobby Jr. capitalizes. Dodging the punch, Bobby Jr. comes forward and hammers Miranda's abdomen with organ-battering blows—left, right, left, right—until the aging fighter collapses against the ropes, prompting the referee to start the count.

"Get up!" Bobby Jr. shouts, his face wild-eyed with adrenaline. "Get up!"

"Eight, nine, ten!" the referee calls, flailing his arms. "It's over!"

Bobby Jr. raises his right arm in the center of the ring, leans back his head, and yells triumphantly. Ducking the ropes, Gunn runs to his kid, taking him by the waist and pulling him high, parading him around the ring while peering into his face as the 1,200-strong crowd shouts, father and son beaming, immersed in the moment, the rest of the world a blur. "My boy made me so proud tonight," Gunn later explains. "I love you, Bobby."

Eight weeks later, the new World Boxing Association rankings were released. Bobby Jr. has progressed to fourteenth in the world's super middleweight rankings. For every boxer, it is a career-defining accomplishment. It's astonishing for someone who has only been trained and guided by his father. "My dad never got the big breaks," Bobby Jr. explains. "Nobody did him no favors." He pauses. "It simply makes me thankful. "I never take anything for granted.

Gunn smiles and merely shakes his head. "Give God the glory," he declares. "My boy is in the world rankings."

It's a frigid morning in November in New Jersey, with temperatures dropping into the forties, and Gunn and his son are celebrating the news by doing what they always do: driving out to pave another driveway in their dual one-ton truck. "I've been working like a dog," Gunn says, blowing steam from a Dunkin' Donuts cup while his French bulldog, Max, rests in his lap. "I am overwhelmed by life, but you know how it goes. "Just trying to get things going."

For Gunn, Bobby Jr.'s victory is the only bright spot in an otherwise bleak year. Since losing to Roy Jones Jr. in February, Gunn has gone back to his typical hustle, laying asphalt and attempting to persuade someone to try bare-knuckle boxing as a sport. As usual, the endeavor has halted. Earlier this year, he and Feldman felt they were close to securing approval for a sanctioned bare-knuckle tournament in a Midwestern state, but the state backed out, and the event never took place. Then, last month, Gunn and Shannon Ritch were in talks to fight in a pay-per-view bare-knuckle combat, maybe on Native American land in the Southwest, but the event fell through due to contract disagreements, leaving both sides unhappy.

"I'm done with Gunn," Rich tweeted. "He backed out and is a pussy."

"Wasters," Gunn responded to his own tweet. "Never had any intentions from the beginning."

However, bare knuckles have been the least of Gunn's problems. In recent months, his father, Robert, has slowly decreased in health, doing little more than trekking to the bar or languishing in his room at the Three Diamond Inn in Niagara Falls, drinking and longing for his wife, Jackie. "A hard life catches up to you," says Jimmy Ruml. "He has arthritis and diabetes, but won't admit it, and his vision isn't great anymore. When we go for a drink, he gets tears in his eyes when talking about Jackie. When she died, it simply killed him.

Although Robert spoke with Bobby Jr. before his championship bout in West Virginia, offering advice over the phone, he did not travel south. So, on a recent morning with a cold wind blowing off Lake

Ontario, Gunn headed north to check on his father. He answered the door to find him intoxicated and unshaven, with his room in disarray. "His eyes were all watered," Gunn says. "He wanted to see his grandson."

Shocked by his father's plight, Gunn gave him a shower, shave, and haircut, and the elderly man recovered as usual—even offering Gunn some praise. "Bobby has a natural ability for bare knuckles," Robert explains. "He grew up in a gypsy lifestyle, has professional expertise, and is a rough-and-tumble man. Now, what his heart desires, my heart desires—we're bringing this back." Robert quickly returns to shape himself with another bar fight. "I might start the Old-Timers Bare-Knuckle Club," he jokes, laughing. "I am seventy-three years old and can screw up most guys. I see these sixty-year-olds in these coffee cafes complaining, 'Jeez, my back, my pain pills.' When I was sixty, I could run five miles and then go out and drink all night. Jesus. "What is wrong with these men?"

Gunn smiles and shakes his head. While he may never understand his father, he is confident that the elderly guy will continue to fight and survive. Bobby Jr., however, is another story. While his kid has performed admirably in the ring, Gunn has grown increasingly concerned about his safety outside of it. In the last year, Bobby Jr. had fallen in love with a teenage Traveler girl, gotten engaged, and, according to tradition, prepared to leave the nest and establish his own family—only to have the entire thing abruptly canceled, allegedly owing to clan disputes.

When asked about it, Bobby Jr. and his father say nothing, with Gunn subsequently tweeting, "I pray that my son gets a good decent Christian girl who is humble, puts God first, and is not materialistic."

Even more concerning has been the call of the underworld. As Bobby Jr. has progressed in the ring, he has received more threats and challenges to compete in bare-knuckle fights in the Traveler world, which Gunn has worked hard to keep his son away from his entire life. While not the mob-run underground that Gunn battled in, the Traveler bare-knuckle world has grown more hazardous in its own right, with conflicts expanding beyond fists and into more lethal terrain fuelled by drugs and alcohol.

According to Gunn, the Travelers' conventional world is deteriorating. At one point, he receives a shaky smartphone video of masked Travelers attacking another Traveler over a rivalry, the marauders wrenching open the man's car door and chopping him with a hatchet, cries filling the air before the screen goes black.

"Things are changing," Gunn says, a smartphone earpiece dangling from his face as he drives, attempting to reach the day's client. "Drugs are taking over many of the young nomadic males. Pills, OxyContin, and heroin. It's really putting the brooms to them. Making them insane. They'll grab a gun and a knife and shoot you faster than they did years before. That is why I am concerned about this individual."

Bobby Jr. shrugs from the backseat, his head down over his smartphone. "Ah, they don't do it around me," he says. "I keep good company."

"The younger generation is a lot more violent," Gunn insists. "There's a whole different attitude amongst them."

"That's more in Delaware," Bobby Jr. says. "Nothing to worry about here."

Nonetheless, Gunn is concerned. As a result, he continues to protect Bobby Jr. from the outside world, claiming that his son is not yet ready to venture out on his own. "He's better with me right now," he says. Others disagree, stating that Gunn is overprotective of Bobby Jr., particularly when it comes to his boxing career. Yes, they say, Gunn has developed an unquestionable talent in the ring, but now it's time to give him over to a professional manager and trainer, someone who does this full-time and can take him to the next level. In short, it's time for Gunn to let his son go.

"I think Bobby is more protective of his son than he needs to be," Joe Mack tells me. "Bobby grew up with no one, thus he is too sensitive to him. But he's just too busy to handle his son's profession."

Gunn dismisses such talk. In fact, in the aftermath of his son's championship title win and the accompanying battle offers from promoters—many of whom, Gunn believes, attempted to rip them off with shady management deals—he has even devised a daring proposal that defies decades of Gunn clan code. He says he loves his son so much that he is willing to offer him the best gift of all: his permission to leave the battle game. "You could slash me, rip my heart out, and I come back and win fights," Gunn jokes. "That's my entire existence. "If you don't have that hunger, you will be hurt." He pauses. "My son has a hunger, but he is appalled by the crowds surrounding the game. Yesterday, he said, 'Dad, you're the world champion, and I have to tell you, I don't want to deal with these guys for the rest of my life. They are scumbags. And he's correct. So, now that bare-knuckle fighting is legal, he may not have to do that. If I can make excellent money and do well, it will be my children's future. That's something I can invest in. Bobby can do whatever he wants in life. I do not tell him to play the fighting game. He's already done well. He is an international contender. So if he walks away, I will support him because I love that boy and understand."

Gunn rubbed his face. Sometimes it all gets to him. Sometimes he just has to go away, to return to the one constant he has known since childhood, the one shelter where all outside worries fall away and he can stare into his opponent's eyes and feel the simple electric pleasure of being alive. It is becoming increasingly difficult to reach that point, let alone enter the ring. When all else fails, he merely puts one mangled foot in front of the other, aiming for the next fight, the next rent check, and the next semester of Charlene's private school tuition.

After all, he's just one battle away from his big break.

CHAPTER 15
THE LAST STAND

*G*unn, 44, is set to face off in the first legal, state-sanctioned bare-knuckle combat in US history. It is being broadcast live around the world on pay-per-view, introducing him and his underground sport to the general public. However, instead of elation, Gunn—middle-aged, broken, and out of shape—feels skepticism. "I didn't have time to properly train," he says, shadowboxing the air and peering at the other fighters in the room, thinking about his younger and heavier opponent, Irineu Beato Costa Jr., a heavyweight boxer from São Paulo, Brazil. "All I do is shovel the asphalt. I'm out of shape, and it shows—I'm getting too old for this nonsense."

Gunn has reason to be concerned. His life has altered dramatically in recent months, causing havoc for him and his beloved family. In November, after years of living with his wife and children in their New Jersey apartment, Gunn abruptly uprooted them, putting his family into his extended-cab pickup truck and drove them west to Phoenix. Previously, Gunn would take his family to Arizona for the winter, leaving the snows of New Jersey to lay asphalt with other travelers in the desert. But this time was different: Gunn and his family were permanently relocating to the west. "I just got sick of New Jersey," he explains, resting on a wooden bench in the backstage locker area. "Too many people are bringing us down." "We needed a new scene."

Gunn claims he and his family left their home in New Jersey due to bare knuckle fighting, with the local fight scene shaking him down to be a part of the new sport that was finally becoming popular. "Guys kept threatening me for money," Gunn explains. "No, I didn't have it. But they thought I said, 'Come on, Bobby, give me five grand or I'll make sure the sport never happens.'"

In actuality, Gunn may have fled New Jersey for a different reason. Bobby Jr.'s engagement to a local Irish Traveler girl fell through in 2017, rocking his family and causing rifts among the Traveler community. Bobby Jr., now 21, was crushed. Gunn, upset by the ordeal, was at a loss. Perhaps the move was supposed to provide a fresh start for everyone. "That was very hard on me," Gunn says of their breakup. "My mind was fried." "Our house was in disarray.

After arriving in Phoenix in November, Gunn and Bobby Jr. got to work, scouring the desert with other Travelers to knock on doors and pave driveways, returning to Rose and Charlene's leased apartment every night. Soon, the family got into a pattern, and everything appeared to return to normal. Then, in March, Gunn awoke to the shock of his life: Bobby Jr. had vanished in the night, fleeing to Las Vegas to elope with a new Traveler girl he had started dating, marrying in a casino without informing anybody. Gunn, who had spent practically every day of his life with Bobby Jr. for the previous 10 years, accompanying him to gyms, fights, and building sites, was distraught. "I was in shock," Gunn remembers. "I was angry. Little Bobby did it without my knowledge—I couldn't believe it.

In April, barely weeks after Bobby Jr.'s elopement, Gunn, Rose, and Charlene faced a decision: should they accompany Bobby Jr. to his new home or go their own way? Bobby Jr. and his fiancée relocated to Baltimore to be closer to her parents' clan following their elopement. As part of his new life, he put his boxing career on hold to work full-time and create his own paving company to support his family. Gunn and his family needed to determine what to do next. For years, Gunn had wished to live and work in Montana, where the clear mountain rivers reminded him of his Canadian upbringing. "My plan was to go to Montana," he says. "It's a beautiful place just across the border from Alberta and Saskatchewan, where my father used to take me as a child. "I wanted to get away from all the craziness and horseshit."

Ultimately, Gunn and Rose opted to keep their family intact. "We moved to Baltimore so my wife could be closer to Bobby Jr.," Gunn tells me. "When you have a chance to be around your kid, then you want to be around them."

As the winter snows melted in May, Gunn and his family relocated to an apartment on the outskirts of Baltimore—a sort of homecoming for the aged fighter. His mother was originally from the area and had been buried there for many years, and her tribe still lived there. After moving his family into an apartment, Gunn began visiting his mother's grave, leaving notes placed within a crucifix on the gravestone, seeking guidance as everything around him seemed to unravel. "God never promises it'll be a bed of roses," he says.

Gunn, now working alone, felt the proximity to his son distressing, a reminder of a truth he had previously overlooked: Bobby Jr. was now ready to strike out on his own. Gunn, who had always attempted to provide Bobby Jr. with the love and security he had never had, found the discovery too difficult to bear. He tried to stay upbeat by messaging Bobby Jr. in the mornings and calling him during breaks on construction sites, but there was no way around it. Gunn was crushed. "I was married young, too," he replies, scratching his face. "So it might help him become a better person." But it also gets me angry. I'm experiencing conflicting emotions."

Without his son, Gunn threw himself into his task, spreading asphalt until far after dark, performing double the effort while his bruised body continued to deteriorate. There was awful news all around him. The son of a Traveler friend was killed in a fiery accident near Brownsville, Texas. All of the tools were stolen from Gunn's truck in a Baltimore parking lot. Alone on employment sites, Gunn stewed, his tweets becoming darker: "Lord, Lord, I need you. "I'm completely alone."

Finally, in April, there was good news: bare-knuckle boxing was back. Throughout 2017, Feldman traveled the country, donning his suit and delivering his PowerPoint presentation on legalizing the gloveless sport to twenty-eight states in a row, only to be denied by every one of them, until Wyoming bit. "The commissioner told me, 'I love two things: fighting and capitalism,'" Feldman echoes. "I finally found my boyfriend. He's a boxer, a former congressman, and a multimillionaire—he's fucking big-time out there!"

Wyoming, a rural state with a strong history of western independence, has a population of 570,000 and is home to cattlemen, Native Americans, and fracking wildcatters who love to defy tradition—a mentality exemplified by Bryan Pedersen, the state athletic commissioner. "I take a lot of pride in the three-oh-seven," Pedersen says, referring to the state's area code, while lifting weights and conversing over a headset in March 2018. "As a rural state, we value our independence. I receive positive feedback from battling. It's a symbol of being Western and tough."

Pedersen, 43, is a former state senator who now works as a financial adviser for RBC Wealth Management in Cheyenne, the state capital, which has a population of 64,000 and is located in the state's flat, windswept southeast. Pedersen, the son of a local RBC consultant whose wife worked on Republican campaigns, including former Vice President Dick Cheney's, has always blended finance and politics with adventure. After graduating from the University of Wyoming with a degree in psychology in 1998, he spent his twenties working in Cheyenne while also running with the bulls in Pamplona, studying French cooking at Le Cordon Bleu in London, and climbing Mount Kilimanjaro in Tanzania—a feat he completed on the same day he learned he had won the Republican primary for state representative in Wyoming at the age of twenty-nine. "There's never a dull moment when you're around Bryan," a friend told an interviewer in 2011. "He makes decisions and then follows through on them. ..He takes on challenges that many people would not even consider."

Fighting, more than anything else, was Pedersen's true passion. Pedersen, a bald, meaty 5'11", 185-pound longtime scrapper, says, "Fighting was something you did for fun in college bars." In his late forties, he began formally studying martial arts to stay in shape. Fixated on the sport, he moved to Bangkok to train Muay Thai kickboxing, and went on to compete in amateur bouts around the West. As a state representative in 2012, he introduced legislation to legalize the sport in Wyoming, establishing the Wyoming State Board of Mixed Martial Arts, the country's first state commission dedicated only to MMA. In 2013, he even put on gloves to compete in the state's first sanctioned pro MMA event, fracturing his nose and injuring himself before losing in front of a crowded arena at Cheyenne Frontier Days Exhibit Hall. "I whipped wholesale buttocks for four minutes and twenty seconds," Pedersen explains. "Then, halfway through the second round, I had a massive adrenaline rush. After that, nothing remained in my body. "So I lost," he says, shrugging. "I left pro fighting to become the commissioner—I'm excited about combat sports."

For years, Pedersen pushed to make MMA a popular sport in Wyoming, attracting promoters with some of the lowest state fees in the country. Despite his attempts, he was constantly met with the same problem: no one wanted to stage events in the country's least populous state—a terrain with fewer population than Washington, DC.

Finally, in 2017, Pedersen saw an opportunity to put Wyoming on the map through an upstart sport that blended his love of adrenaline with spectacle and profit: bare knuckle. "In Wyoming, we are driven by an independent western spirit," according to Pedersen. "And I'm looking to bring money to my state by taking this mainstream."

In reality, Pedersen intended to authorize bare knuckle for another reason: the sport was already allowed and performed in his jurisdiction. In 2012, by establishing an MMA commission rather than a pro boxing commission, which would have barred the sport, Pederson effectively legalized bare knuckle fighting in Wyoming. In response, Corey Williams, a general contractor in the six-hundred-person town of Shoshoni, organized bare-knuckle events across the state, including modest affairs with local fighters in venues like town halls.

Although lawful, bare-knuckle fights were not sanctioned because Pedersen has never officially acknowledged the sport. "People found loopholes," he says. "By not making it unlawful, we have made the sport legal. So individuals put on tiny shows all across the state."

Bare-knuckle fighting eventually gained unfavorable attention in Wyoming, and police chiefs and city councils fought to prevent it from happening. In 2015, after a bare-knuckle fighter was hospitalized with jaw injuries at one of Williams' bouts in Riverton, the local city administrator, acting on a recommendation from the chief of police, called for the sport to be banned. The Riverton city council soon began working on an ordinance to outlaw the sport. Williams filed federal lawsuits in response, and the entire ordeal became an issue for the state commission. ("I wasn't in violation of any laws," Williams says.) Finally, in 2017, when Feldman arrived with his tightly run format of bare knuckle, Pedersen saw an opportunity—a chance to sanction a sport that was already taking place in his state while also making international headlines, kicking off combat sports in Wyoming.

In December 2017, Pedersen and Feldman began trying to make bare knuckle boxing a sanctioned sport, doing everything they could to make it safe despite the fact that it would face scrutiny. Feldman collaborated with Pedersen, state politicians, and outside experts to create a forty-two-page rulebook. He stealthily secured the intellectual property rights to numerous names for bare knuckles, guaranteeing that he would own every aspect of the sport and anticipating rival leagues to emerge in his wake. He also designed and copyrighted a $140,000 ten-ton steel arena, a "squared circle" made up of a twenty-two-foot-wide ring within a thirty-foot square—an engineering marvel unlike any other fight arena in existence.

Technically designating bare knuckle as a sort of MMA—the only type of sport he could legally oversee—Pedersen assisted Feldman in moving it through the Wyoming government, making a basic presentation to lawmakers at each stage. "We already regulate MMA and kickboxing," Pedersen explains. "In both of those sports you can take a shinbone to the head, which is like getting hit with a baseball bat." He says. "Much of the sanctioning and legality of bare-knuckle fighting stems from a misunderstanding. Some argue that bare knuckle boxing is equivalent to boxing without gloves, which would make it illegal in most states. However, the regulations for bare-knuckle fighting differ. They enable striking as well as other types of techniques such as Muay Thai clinches. So, the sport has been misconstrued. It's called bare-knuckle boxing. But in reality, it is bare-knuckle fighting."

Feldman finally received the long-awaited call in March 2018. Wyoming became the first state in the nation to recognize bare-knuckle boxing. Feldman tried to keep calm while driving his beat up SUV in Philadelphia. But, after over a decade of trying to make the sport a reality, he couldn't stop himself. "I tried to be nice but eventually said, 'Fuck that. "I'm jumping out of my skin," Feldman remembers. "I literally yelled, 'Fucking yes, guy!'"

Feldman felt he had just been granted a once-in-a-lifetime opportunity that might propel him from the monotony of low-level promotions to global stardom. He had a financial backing (an unnamed angel investor from Philadelphia), a state license, and decades of fight promotion experience. He now faced only one final challenge: to put on a pioneering event, one that had never been done before in US history, one that featured good fights without serious injury, and one that would create a new sport and multimillion-dollar company. If he succeeds, he may be set for life. If he failed, he would be forced to return to his anonymous day-to-day promotions, and he may face criminal charges if a fighter was gravely injured. On top of everything, Feldman had one lingering concern: would bare knuckle remain compelling after it was removed from the underground?

Feldman realized that only one man could actually assist him pull it off.

"I've got to pee again," Gunn says, waddling to the urinal while wearing only his padded groin cup, underwear, and boxing shoes. "My God, I sound like a grandfather."

Gunn, battle-scarred, out-of-shape, and with a huge prostate, finishes up and returns to the Cheyenne Ice and Events Center's backstage dressing area. It's Saturday, June 2, 2018, and the evening's ten-card event has already begun beyond the concrete walls of the dressing room, with over two thousand beer-drinking, cowboy-hat-wearing locals yelling for blood, their yells and stomping boot heels rocking the stadium like thunder. Inside the dressing area, however, the mood is muted as boxers prepare for their battles by punching air, disappearing inside their headphones, or reciting prayers, with numerous smartphone boomboxes blasting everything from Elvis to Nas. Overall, the room is tense, with pro fighters long accustomed to entering the ring but never without gloves—except for one man, whom they all admire: Gunn. "I'm so happy I get to see you fight," says a tattooed young fighter. Gunn smiles. "God bless you," he said. "This is my last one—I'm the oldest fighter here."

Tonight, Gunn is making his final stand. The legend will fight his final bout in an ice-and-roller-skating arena decorated with giant American flags and construction company advertisements, alongside nineteen other fighters from pro boxing, MMA, and street brawling, all vying to resurrect one of America's oldest sports. The ten-card event, which was attended by cheering cowboys, farmers, oil-rig workers, and uniformed soldiers, featured a mix of up-and-coming contenders like former UFC star Bec Rawlings and aging pros like former UFC heavyweight Ricco Rodriguez, all fighting in five two-minute rounds while wearing nothing on their hands but wrapping about an inch below the knuckle. The setting is a sort of promenade of broken-bodied fantasies. B-list veterans like 41-year-old former army boxer and MMA fighter Eric Prindle, looking for one last chance at glory, compete against utter unknowns like 33-year-old stonemason Sam Shewmaker from the Missouri Ozarks, dressed in US flag trunks and a philosopher's beard.

Only one thing is certain: nobody knows what to anticipate. "You guys are making history," one of the referees, Dan Miragliotta, tells the collected crowd of fighters before the show, as everyone huddles in a quiet corner and yells for the bouts to begin. "You're pioneers."

Dave Feldman, dressed in a blue suit and an open white collared shirt, then issues a more forthright ultimatum. "If you don't put up a good fight, you're not getting paid," he jokes. "If you show some fucking heart, though, that's different—you're getting a bonus."

Gunn is now ready, just minutes before his bout. Backstage in the locker room, he is approached by a continual stream of boxers, some of whom want to clasp hands in prayer, while others seek advice. While all of the fighters have experience with gloved combat, none have competed much in bare knuckle, thus they are all attempting to gather some last-minute information. Rodriguez, the former UFC heavyweight champion, discusses body shot strategy with Gunn. "I used to spar with Bobby ten years ago in Bayonne, New Jersey," Rodriguez tells me. "He would clobber me and then take me aside to demonstrate tricks. "He is a legend."

Maurice Jackson, a professional MMA fighter from Las Vegas, smiles as he comes to the locker room following his fight. In less than a minute, he finished off his opponent with a left hook and two right crosses. "Bobby, I did what you said," Jackson adds, smiling. "I tapped him with the reach, and he said, 'Oh, shit'—it worked!"

Gunn grinned. "I gave advice to both him and his opponent," said the politician. "Only one listened."

Gunn, the grizzled YouTube legend, smiles, playing the role of an elder statesman. Inside, however, he is a wreck. "I don't like the air up here," he admits, breathing heavily in the 6,000-foot atmosphere while tying tape and gauze across his wrists, the only permitted hand protection for the event. "And I don't enjoy packaging. They don't do any good anyway—I like old school."

Gunn has struggled in recent weeks. In addition to pouring asphalt six days a week, he has been actively advertising this event, tweeting and giving interviews to sources such as SiriusXM, Men's Health, and ESPN. Then, on Wednesday, he flew to Denver and drove 100 miles north to Cheyenne to continue the press tour, smiling for days alongside Feldman, Pedersen, and the other nineteen social-media combatants.

In many ways, Gunn finds all of this satisfying, as the world finally catches up with him and the sport he has been practicing for decades. But it's also exhausting. Earlier this week, while driving his truck to Cheyenne, seeing the interminable wind farms, pumpjacks, and booze stores of the Great Plains, he experienced a loss of confidence—a sentiment shared by Feldman. Following his loss against Roy Jones Jr. last year, Gunn is widely regarded as a washed-up boxer. He is now the defending bare-knuckle champion. He's not even fighting as the main event, but in a middle-of-the-card contest. Gunn's face rarely appears on the posters.

"I feel kind of weird headlining," Rodriguez confesses at one point. "Bobby is the defending champion."

Gunn is painfully unsure of himself, having wrecked his body and lost his compass. When he is not smiling for the cameras, he has been pacing incessantly, bemoaning the loss of his kid and his beloved bulldog, Max, who has remained with Rose and Charlene. In addition, he is concerned about preserving his final tangible asset: his perfect 72-0 bare-knuckle record. "Don't I look better than some of these guys?" He mumbles to himself at one point, rolling his stump-like neck. "I simply can't think about the fight. What is the point? "Whatever happens, will happen."

Gunn is completely focused on the fight. He believes he has little chance of defeating his opponent, Costa, a younger, stronger 6'3", 200-pound boxer with seventeen knockouts in his last twenty-six fights. Gunn also dislikes the event's general setup. In addition to wearing wrist wraps as a safety precaution to prevent broken hands, he must battle in the event's fast-paced two-minute bouts. It's a departure from his customary underground fights, which have no time limit and allow him to assess his opponent before going for the kill. In response, Gunn developed a basic technique over the phone with his father in Niagara Falls. It's equivalent to a Hail Mary. He'll come in quickly and close to Costa, hoping for a quick knockout before the monster can demolish him with his greater reach.

"I'm gonna roll the dice," Gunn declares, writing the name of his recently deceased Traveler friend on his chest and dedicating the fight to him. "Go in close and chop him up like a lawnmower—it's my only chance."

"You are up next, Bobby!"

Gunn starts to pace. Wearing a black sleeveless shirt, black shorts, and black shoes, he favors his right foot, which was damaged by a rooftop fall. As a final reminder of his worries, he unzipped his gym bag and discovered that his wife, Rose, had packed his son's gear instead of his own. After immersing the smaller mouth guard in boiling water and inserting it into his mouth—grimacing as the hot rubber molded to his teeth—Gunn had slid into Bobby Jr. 's cup and shoes, the smaller garments adding to his pain. "Bobby Jr. usually packs my bag," he explains. "I miss him."

Gunn exits the backstage dressing area and walks through the concrete tunnel to the ring. Unlike most other fighters, he does not have a trainer or manager. Instead, he is approached by a camera crew looking for a quick interview, followed by a group of fighters asking for selfies. But as he gets to his position in the wings, Gunn is alone. He withdraws within himself, allowing the outer world to fade away, going through the same motions that have supported him from boyhood, the mantra he has always repeated like an omen. "I'm the boss," he exclaims, punching the air.

Sure, he wants to win the first state-sanctioned bare-knuckle boxing event in US history, cementing his position in the record books and legitimizing a shaky career. But, as usual, Gunn fights for a different cause. Since Bobby Jr.'s departure, he has shifted his focus to his children's personal objectives. So today, while shadowboxing in the air, the crowd yelling just beyond the darkness, Gunn concentrates on his one true motivation: to take the $10,000 prize money home to his daughter, Charlene, who, he now claims, can defy Traveler custom and attend private school into her teens. "She's a smart girl, the joy of my heart," he tells me. "I want her to go to school for as long as she wants."

"Just one minute, Bobby!"

Gunn jumps from foot to foot, opening and closing his mouth while looking at the ring in the limelight. Suddenly, he is challenged by a man, who is coming up in his face and whispering in his ear: Feldman. The duo's journey to this moment has been long and often fraught with struggle. Although Gunn introduced Feldman to the sport and has helped him build it over the years, it is unclear whether the aged fighter has a formal ownership in Feldman's firm, Bare Knuckle Fighting Championships, which is organizing the event.

Feldman understands, however, that he requires Gunn's assistance. Twenty-five years ago, just down the road in Denver, the UFC created history by hosting its inaugural PPV fighting event, a bloody wild affair that was dismissed by the world before growing to become a $12 billion cultural juggernaut. Feldman, wearing his murdered father's necklace beneath his suit, sees this as an opportunity for bare-knuckle fighting—and he needs his star fighter to carry off one last triumph.

"We worked a long time," Feldman whispers, his lips on Gunn's ear. "Now is your fucking moment. Go out there and do what you need to do. Do not be safe. Do not box. Don't be technical; just go knock this fucking man out."

Gunn sniffles.

"All right."

The stage becomes dark. The aged combatant takes a final long breath. "I'm the boss, I'm the boss, I'm the boss," Gunn tells himself, "Come on, big fucker, let's go."

Walking out to Whitesnake's "Here I Go Again" in front of a frenzied crowd, Gunn takes the stage and faces Costa, a musclebound opponent who looms over him. Standing mere feet apart, the men raise their hands. It is a remarkable sight in American sports history: sans boxing gloves.

"Knuckle up!" One of the two referees yells.

Gunn charges Costa and delivers a powerful left hook to the liver, dropping him within seconds. "Down, Costa!The announcer yells. The audience cheers.

Gunn, now enthusiastic and dancing on his feet, circles the ring while Costa attempts a weak ascent. Gunn seizes the opportunity and attacks him once more. Costa delivers a punch. Gunn ducks and leans forward, this time aiming for the kill with another deep shot to the liver, followed by a last overhand right punch to the temple as he falls.

The audience roars.

Costa lies collapsed on the ring.

The struggle is over.

"That left hook to the liver—Ouch! That was a nasty shot," the announcer says. "That takes your breath and your legs away, immediately."

In barely forty-one seconds, Gunn demonstrated why he is the sport's champion, demolishing his opponent with the accuracy of a surgeon, the victory and body shots so swift that the Internet will wonder how he did it. But for Gunn, it's simply another win to add to his 72-0 bare-knuckle record, this time with a critical twist: he won in a legal arena in front of a pay-per-view audience all across the world, making history. "Just like that, the legacy continues," says the announcer. "The legend that is bare-knuckle fighter Bobby Gunn."

Gunn lifts his arms triumphantly, smiling and squinting at the lights.